Values in English Language Teaching

Values in English Language Teaching

Bill Johnston
Indiana University

LEA 2003

LAWRENCE ERLBAUM ASSOCIATES, PUBLISHERS
Mahwah, New Jersey   London

Lawrence Erlbaum Associates, Inc., Publishers
10 Industrial Avenue
Mahwah, NJ 07430

Cover design by Kathryn Houghtaling Lacey

Library of Congress Cataloging-in-Publication Data

Johnston, Bill.
Values in English language teaching / Bill Johnston.
    p. cm.
Includes bibliographical references (p.) and index.
ISBN 0-8058-4293-4 (cloth : alk. Paper)
ISBN 0-8058-4294-2 (pbk : alk. paper)
    1. English language—Study and teaching—Foreign speakers—
Moral and ethical aspects.
    2. English teachers—Professional ethics. I. Title.

PE1128.A2 J+

                                        2002023551
                                              CIP
Books published by Lawrence Erlbaum Associates are printed on acid-
free paper, and their bindings are chosen for strength and durability.

Printed in the United States of America
10 9 8 7 6 5 4 3 2

For Ned

Contents

Preface

English language teaching (ELT) is not merely a matter of training students in a particular set of skills. Rather, the occupation of ELT is profoundly imbued with values, and these values furthermore are complex and riven with dilemmas and conflict. This book offers an extended analysis of the values underlying our work in ELT. I believe many teachers will find that what I have to say resonates with their own experiences and their own views; I hope this is so, and I do not believe that what I write here is "new" in the sense that no one has thought it before. However, from my knowledge of the literature of ELT it seems that these matters are rarely if ever raised in print in the professional dialogue of our field, and they are certainly not given the sustained attention they deserve.

In a way, the book falls under the category of philosophy of education. However, this is not the dry, abstract philosophy with which the word is often associated. The philosophical analysis in this book is built around real-life dilemmas faced by language teachers in a variety of settings. My aim is to produce what might be called a practical philosophy of language teaching, in which abstract conceptualizations not only relate to, but actually arise from, real situations.

This book is written above all for English language teachers. Although I hope that what I have to say will influence researchers, administrators, policymakers, and especially teacher educators, my primary audience are those who actually teach English as a second or foreign language. I hope this book will appeal to thinking teachers who are continually striving to understand their own classrooms. However, I do not offer neat, ready-made solutions to language teaching problems. My work is in the spirit of what Edge (2001b) wrote in the context of action research: "The thinking teacher is no longer perceived as someone who applies theories, but as someone who theorizes practice" (p. 6). The perspective on ELT that I set out in this book is intended not as a theory to be applied but as a framework to help teachers theorize their own work.

In an effort to address as wide a spectrum of teachers as possible in the field, I use the term *English language teaching*, or *ELT*, in this book. There are by now dozens of acronyms in the field (ESL, EFL, ENL, ESOL, EAL, TEFL, etc.), and *ELT* is intended to subsume all of these, in particular the frequently made distinction between English as a second language (ESL)—the teaching of English in settings where English alone is the dominant language—and English as a foreign language (EFL)—the teaching of English in countries where other languages are dominant. *ELT* also includes those considerable swathes of the world (like India and Pakistan) in which the ESL–EFL distinction is problematic. What I have to say should be interesting and relevant to teachers of English in all kinds of contexts.

I have deliberately used the feminine pronouns *she* and *her* to refer to teachers, because most of the teachers I know are women. I'm sure my male readers will not mind substituting *he* and *him* where appropriate—or, better still, considering themselves included in the category of *her,* just as women have had to do with male pronouns for many centuries now.

A crucial issue in language teaching and in teacher development is that of *voice*. Both as a researcher and as a teacher educator, my primary interest is in language teachers. At the same time, I want to talk *to* teachers and *with* them, not *for* them—I don't want to usurp their voice. For that reason, wherever possible I have used the actual words of teachers in describing the various moral dilemmas that arise in their work. I have tried to include the voices of teachers from different countries and working in different contexts, to make the point that the moral dynamics I discuss are in some form or another common to all ELT situations. All the situations and stories found in this book are real; I have not made up any examples to prove a point. Where examples are taken from published—that is, public—work, I use the authors' names. Where they are from private sources—student journals, e-mails, or conversations—I have used pseudonyms. In some cases I have altered certain details of stories to protect the confidentiality of those concerned.

The assumption underlying what I write is that *all* aspects of language teaching are imbued with values and moral meaning. In this book, however, I concentrate on exploring the moral significance of certain specific aspects of language teaching, chapter by chapter.

In chapter 1 I set out the basic claim that I substantiate throughout the book: that ELT is a value-laden occupation; that the values underlying it are complex, conflicting, and rooted in the details of context; and that it is important to bring to consciousness the moral dimensions of English teaching. I also set out basic definitions and understandings of terms such as *values* and *morality*, and I describe the philosophical underpinnings of my work, especially the writings of Nel Noddings (1984). I end by surveying existing research on the moral dimensions of teaching in general education and by suggesting that in some ways ELT is comparable but that in others it has its own peculiar moral landscape that must be explored and understood on its own terms.

In chapter 2 I examine the moral dimensions of ELT classroom interaction. This includes things that teachers and students say and do, the ways in which they interact, and the materials they use. I begin by taking a detailed look at the moral meanings encoded in examples of classroom discourse, focusing on four aspects: rules and regulations, curricular substructure, expressive morality, and voice. I then look at three aspects of the ELT curriculum that are charged with values: values in the textbook, moral choices that have to be made in pronunciation teaching, and the clash of values that underlies the process–product debate in the teaching of writing. Last, I analyze an important yet often overlooked moral dynamic: the clash between the teacher's role as individual and teacher and her position as de facto representative of the institution in and for which she teaches.

In chapter 3 I explore a matter close to my heart: the moral side of the politics of language teaching. In this chapter I focus in particular on critical pedagogy, on the moral meanings it encodes, and the dilemmas of values to which it gives rise. After first providing evidence to support the claim that all teaching is political, I briefly outline the tenets of critical pedagogy. I analyze the moral aspects of an example of critical pedagogy in action in an ESL setting, and then I consider the moral underpinnings of the question of whether critical pedagogy can be enacted in EFL contexts. After presenting a short critique of critical pedagogy from the standpoint of values, I analyze the central moral dilemma that dwells in the political dimension of ELT: the clash between the good inherent in the act of teaching someone another language and our participation through this teaching in global processes of cultural, linguistic, and economic imperialism.

Chapter 4 is devoted to an in-depth analysis of the moral significance of one aspect of teachers' work: that of testing and assessment. I begin by considering the value-laden nature of evaluation. I then look at the moral dimensions of widely accepted forms of student evaluation practiced in ELT programs. I move on to consider the issues of values raised by standardized tests such as the Test of English as a Foreign Language (TOEFL) and the moral dilemmas that inhere in alternative forms of assessment. I end by posing the question of whether morally justifiable forms of evaluation are possible.

In chapter 5 I consider three facets of teacher identity which are particularly tightly bound up with values and moral judgment. The first of these is the teacher–student relation: specifically, the ways in which the personal lives of students impinge willy-nilly on our professional relations with them, and also the tension between authority and solidarity in relations with students. Second, I look at professionalism and the clashes of values that arise from teachers' attempts to assume an identity as a professional. Last, I consider the place of religious beliefs in language teaching, both from the point of view of the teacher's own religious values and what these mean for her actions, and from the perspective of different and clashing religious views held by students.

Chapter 6 concerns the moral dimension of language teacher development. In this chapter I begin by arguing that teacher development itself represents and embodies a particular set of values. Next, I consider the values implicit in the practice of teacher research—that is, investigations of teaching initiated and led by teachers themselves—and I take a close look at two examples of teacher research that focus on moral meanings in the classroom. I then reflect on the role of values in teacher career development, in particular the clashes of values that accompany important career decisions. Next I discuss the moral dimensions of the marginality experienced by many in ELT and the need for advocacy for teachers. I close by considering some of the consequences of my perspective on language teaching for the practice of teacher education.

The final chapter, 7, constitutes a taking stock in which I reflect on the significance of the analysis presented in this book for the practice of language teaching. In particular, I revisit and summarize the principal moral dilemmas of the field that I have identified throughout the book; consider the foundational values underlying our decision making in situations of moral dilemmas; and revisit the teacher–student relation, the core of the moral life of the ELT classroom.

Many people have helped in the writing of this book. First and foremost I want to thank Julian Edge, whose own moral courage has been an inspiration to me for many years now, and whose friendship is one of the most treasured things I have been given in my years in the field. His belief in this project and his close reading of drafts of the manuscript were invaluable.

This book began a long time ago as an unfinished project with a graduate colleague of mine at the University of Hawaiʻi, Enid Mok. Enid, wherever you are, thank you.

I owe a large debt of gratitude to those people who have shared my interest in the moral dimensions of teaching. Above all I thank Cary Buzzelli for being a wonderful colleague and friend and for getting me started on writing about this topic (and not letting me stop), and for his comments on an early draft. I also want to thank Beverly Ruiz, Andrea Juhász, and Jim Marken, and the other members of the "Morality Club" of 1996, for working with me.

For their very helpful feedback on earlier versions of the text, I thank Stephanie Vandrick, Pia Moriarty, and Kim Johnson.

I wish to express my particular gratitude to Naomi Silverman, a paragon among editors. Naomi, thank you for your belief in this project from beginning to end and for your hard work in shaping the manuscript along the way. You made all the difference.

My great thanks go to my colleagues and former and present students for sharing their stories with me.

Last, but certainly not least, I thank my wife, Kasia Rydel-Johnston, without whom, for any number of reasons, I could not have written this book.

—Bill Johnston

1

The Teacher as Moral Agent

English language teaching (ELT), that is, the teaching of English as a second or foreign language, is usually portrayed in the professional literature as being primarily concerned with the mental acquisition of a language. This book offers an alternative perspective. My central thesis here is that in fact language teaching and learning are shot through with values, and that language teaching is a profoundly value-laden activity. This thesis can be broken down into three basic ideas.

1. The essence of language teaching, like the essence of all teaching, lies in values: That is, it is moral in nature. I define exactly what I mean by *moral* later in this chapter.
2. The morality of teaching is highly complex, paradoxical, and saturated with important and difficult dilemmas.
3. The moral dimension of teaching has rarely been talked about, and most of the time teachers are not consciously aware of it; yet there is a great need to uncover and examine the values that inform teaching, in the interests both of the professional development of teachers and of the practice of language teaching.

The main purpose of this book is to explore the specific ways in which values underlie various aspects of language teaching. I look at what those values are, explicate the moral dilemmas that we as teachers face at every step, and suggest ways of thinking about these dilemmas that may help teachers to deal with them.

I begin this chapter with a real-life story that exemplifies the kinds of dilemmas I am talking about. I use the story to introduce some of the beliefs and values that underlie what I have to say in this book. The rest of the chapter lays the groundwork for what follows. I first outline my understanding of the nature of morality in teaching, and I explain how morality relates to values, ethics, and ideology. I describe what I see as the limitations of the majority of philosophical analyses and introduce the work of Nel Noddings and Zygmunt Bauman as central in my own philosophical foundations. I proceed to survey what has been written about the morality of teaching both in general education and in ELT, and I enumerate some of the particular moral issues that distinguish our field from other educational settings.

Without further ado, let me open the discussion with an example of the kinds of moral dilemmas I will be investigating throughout the book.

INTRODUCTION: PETER'S STORY

Some years ago my friend Peter was teaching English to a senior class of Palestinian and Jordanian students in a college of education in Jordan. One of his students was uncooperative and unfriendly; despite both encouragement and warnings, he did little work and made hardly any progress. When the end of the year came, and following a dismal performance on the final examination, Peter did not hesitate to give this student a failing grade. After Peter had completed his grading, he met with the head of his department to go over the grades assigned. When the case of the weak student came up, there was a long silence. The head of department eventually said something like, "Well, if that's the grade you've assigned ... ." There was another silence. Peter asked what he meant. The head of department explained, all the while asserting his respect for Peter's decision, that a failing grade would mean that this student, a Palestinian from the occupied West Bank who had been away from his family for 4 years, would now have to return to Israel and would not be allowed to leave the country again. His chances for employment would be severely affected. "However, this is your decision," said the head of department. Peter resolutely refused to change the grade, saying, rightly, that the student did not deserve a higher grade. A series of long, uncomfortable silences ensued. At no point did the head of department threaten or challenge Peter. In the end, however, Peter changed his mind and gave the student a passing grade.

This story is an example of the centrality of values in second language teaching. I believe that every teacher will recognize in this story the elements of situations they themselves have experienced. In a literal sense, many of us have found ourselves giving a student a grade different from that which the student deserved. More generally, I believe that every one of us has experienced situations in which the values that we hold turn out to be in conflict. (Incidentally, though I have changed Peter's name, this story, and every other example given in this book, is taken from real life. I have not made up any examples for the purpose of illustrating a point—rather, I have taken the stories themselves as starting points.)

In this particular story, it seems to me that two of Peter's most profoundly held beliefs are in conflict. On the one hand, he holds a professional belief (which I think many teachers will recognize and share) that it is right and good to give students a score or grade that accurately represents their level of achievement, and that it is morally wrong to give a student a grade (whether higher or lower) that he or she does not deserve. But another value that Peter holds dear (and which I would also want to claim for my own) is that, whether as a teacher or as a person, it is good to help others in whatever way one can, and it is bad to create problems for someone or cross his or her plans when one is in a position to be of assistance. In the story about the Palestinian student, these two values are in conflict; whatever the solution, Peter's values will be denied in some way. In addition, of course, this rendering of the issue is grossly oversimplistic. In reality, Peter found himself dealing with a vast array of factors, including the personality of the student in question, his relations with his director, his relations with his other students, and the entire complexity of the social and political context.[1]

For me, stories such as this one go to the very heart of the work of teaching. I am fascinated by this kind of story, and I have found that other teachers too find them compelling; they somehow capture a deeply meaningful aspect of what we do. Yet although many, many teachers I have spoken to remember incidents like this with extraordinary clarity and regard them as crucial in their own professional development, such stories, and

---

[1]This reading of the situation, of course, is my own. This fact was brought home to me when I showed Peter a draft of this chapter. While acknowledging that I was entitled to my own interpretation, Peter stated clearly that "I don't recognize the second value that you name as one that was on my mind in that situation." He went on to say that reading my account of his dilemma led him to reflect further on the incident and that his own view of it now is as follows:

I was unsure of my right to insist on the primacy of a principle that I had been brought up to believe in, in the face of a moral, social, and political context that was too big and unfamiliar for me to claim knowledge of. I felt inadequate to insist on doing what I thought to be right in the context of what I did not know. If I were to be accused of bottling it, ducking the virtuous act for the popular one, I could not credibly defend myself. From that perspective, I used my ignorance to excuse myself doing an easy wrong. I certainly cannot claim to have served the Palestinian cause by facilitating the qualification of a morose, antisocial and, as far as I could tell, unintelligent youth as a language teacher. The kinder light on the situation is that I paused long enough to entertain the doubt that the cultural and educational certainties of a 21-year-old Brit might not encompass the basis for all actions across the world and, having paused, the doubt won the day.

I cite Peter's reflections at such length both because they are intrinsically of great value and because they remind me of how hard it can be to speak for others accurately and fairly.

the conflicts of values they raise, are never mentioned in books on language teaching methodology—for example, the kinds of books one reads and studies in methods courses during teacher education programs. These books show us good ways to encourage fluency in our students, teach us useful techniques for reading activities or how to use video, and help us think about motivating our learners, but they never address the kinds of tough decision that Peter faced.

Part of the reason for this is that it is very hard to write or speak about such situations. They are highly complex and fraught with ambiguities; furthermore, unlike certain aspects of language pedagogy, it is impossible to produce generalized solutions—each individual situation has to be understood in its own terms. Moreover, in most situations of this kind the application of logic or of "scientific" knowledge is of limited use. To put it plainly, no amount of empirical research will ever answer the question of what Peter should have done. The solution has to be an individual one, dependent on this particular teacher in this particular context, and it rests ultimately not on logic or propositional knowledge but on *belief*: the teacher's belief that he is doing the right thing.

I believe that this kind of story is in fact central to language teaching and to the lives of teachers. Important as teaching methods are, teaching is not ultimately just about methods or the efficient psycholinguistic learning of the language by students. Rather, as Peter's story suggests, it is about our relation with our students as people, with the way we treat them. I have been a teacher myself for twenty years now; the more I teach, and the more I work with teachers and talk with them, the more firmly I have come to the conviction that what we do in classrooms (and outside of them) is fundamentally rooted in the values we hold and in the relation we have with our students.

In this book, then, I aim to explore this dimension of language teaching, which is central to our work but has gone largely ignored until now. I look at the ways in which values, and clashes of values, inhere in everything we do as teachers. I try to provide a language with which to talk about these values and these clashes. And I will encourage you, the reader, to become aware of the values implicit in your own work and to examine these values critically in light of your teaching situation.

The topics I raise in this book are very difficult and very personal; they are likely, as the phrase has it, to push some buttons. I make no apology for this, because I believe that, although these are difficult and controversial issues, they are also essential for a full understanding of our work as language teachers. I believe that a significant part of professional growth comes from the courage to tackle difficult topics, for these are often also the topics that are most important to us. This book is my attempt to sustain such an engagement and to share it with fellow professionals.

At the same time, I acknowledge that my own take on these matters—for example, on situations such as Peter's dilemma, or the many other stories I tell in this book—is highly personal. I want to state clearly that I do not have an agenda in terms of specific values; I do not write from a particular religious or ethical standpoint. I simply believe that these matters are worth talking about. My agenda, then, is to open up aspects of our work to discussion that I believe have been ignored until now in the professional discourse of ELT. In this book I suggest many aspects of language teaching that I believe you ought to think *about*, but I will not tell you *what* to think about them. In doing so I also wish to try to reclaim the use of the term *moral* by those of us who think in moral terms yet do not necessarily align ourselves with particular religious or political factions. My goal is to reveal the value-laden nature of our work in the language classroom and to provide tools for analyzing that work. It is my firm belief that each individual teacher must face her own moral dilemmas in her own way. By the same token, I am not recommending or arguing for any particular teaching methodology but for a way of *seeing* the classroom. Whether change follows as a result of this different way of seeing is a matter for the individual teacher to know.

To state my basic case very briefly, language teaching, like all other teaching, is fundamentally moral, that is, value laden, in at least three crucial ways. First, teaching is rooted in relation, above all the relation between teacher and student; and relation, in turn—the nature of our interactions with our fellow humans—is essentially moral in character. This was seen clearly in Peter's dilemma. Second, all teaching aims to change people; any attempt to change another person has to be done with the assumption, usually implicit, that the change will be for the better.[2] Matters of what is good and bad, better or worse, are moral matters. Third, although "science" in the form of research in various disciplines (second language acquisition, education, sociology, etc.) can give us some pointers, in the overwhelming majority of cases it cannot tell us exactly how to run our class. Thus, the decisions we make as teachers—what homework to assign, how to grade student writing, what to do about the disruptive student in the back row—ultimately also have to be based on moral rather than objective or scientific principles: That is, they have to based on what we believe is right and good—for each stu-

---

[2]This is an educational application of Aristotle's claim, in the *Nicomachean Ethics*, that "every art and every inquiry, and similarly every action and pursuit, is thought to aim at some good" (Aristotle, 1926, p. 1).

dent, for the whole class, and sometimes for ourselves. I elaborate on each of these arguments in the course of the book; each, I believe, applies to teaching in general. In addition, as I explain later, language teaching in particular has its own characteristic moral issues with which to deal.

THE NATURE OF MORALITY IN TEACHING

Before I go on, I should clarify what I mean by *morality*. This is a notoriously difficult and dangerous term, all the more so because it is used so widely, and, as with any term or concept, once academics get their hands on it the picture becomes even murkier.

In this book I shall follow my earlier work on morality in teaching (e.g., Buzzelli & Johnston, 2002). I use *morality* to refer to that (whether more or less coherent) set of a person's beliefs which are evaluative in nature, that is, which concern matters of what is good and what is bad, what is right and what is wrong. I further take morality to be both individual and social. It is individual in that all moral beliefs are mediated through particular people—there is no "morality" without it being instantiated by individuals. It is social in two important senses. First, strong social forces operate on individual moralities, in the form of religious, political, and other beliefs that are shared to a greater or lesser extent by groups of people and encoded in various forms—for example, in religious texts. Second, although the moral values that a person holds may in some abstract sense be independent of those around her, in practice our morality becomes interesting only when our values are played out in social settings—when our inner beliefs are converted into actions that affect others.

Rather than worrying about the extent to which morality is individual or social—that is, seeing this as an either–or choice—I suggest that in fact morality exists precisely in the interplay between the personal and the social.

In this respect, my vision of morality is reminiscent of recent accounts of culture (e.g., Holland, Lachicotte, Skinner, & Cain, 1998; Strauss & Quinn 1997) in which culture, traditionally an impersonal thing outside the individual, is instead seen as both a cognitive and a social force. Strauss and Quinn (1997), for example, argued that cultural meanings cannot be explained "unless we see them as created and maintained in the interaction between the extrapersonal and intrapersonal realms" (p. 8); they wrote further that although "the dynamics of these realms are different," the boundary between them is very much "permeable" (p. 8). My view of morality offers a parallel with Strauss and Quinn's vision of cultural meanings: I see morality as neither a purely individual nor a purely social phenomenon but as existing at the meeting point between the individual and the social, of cognition and community. Furthermore, also like culture, it is not a fixed set of values but, while it may have certain relatively firmly anchored points, to a significant extent it is negotiated both within the individual and between individuals. This was clearly the case in Peter's dilemma: His decision was a moral one, but it emerged from the interplay between the beliefs and values that he brought to the situation and a highly complex set of factors arising from the social and political environment in which he found himself.

This brings me to another characteristic of morality as I conceive it in this book. Although certain beliefs may be absolute, I see most moral issues (dilemmas, conflicts, problems) as being fundamentally dependent on context; that is, because morality exists at the intersection between inner beliefs and social situations, the nature of those situations is of crucial importance. I follow Nel Noddings (1984) in believing that morality is deeply colored by "the uniqueness of human encounters" (p. 5). In this book, the discussion of moral values centers around real-life situations from the work of language teachers. I believe strongly that morality cannot in any interesting or meaningful sense be reduced to unconditional rules of the type "always do X" or "one should never do X to Y."

Let me give an example of the way in which moral judgments are fundamentally affected by context. A few years ago, a Korean woman whom I will call Hae-young took my methods class. Hae-young chose to write her final paper on whole-language instruction. Though I take a process-writing approach with assignments such as this one, Hae-young was very late in giving me even the first draft; it was almost the end of the semester. The paper she gave me was perhaps two thirds taken word for word from the sources she had used, often without acknowledgment. In other words, it seemed to be a clear case of plagiarism. I had encountered a similarly egregious case a couple of years before, in which a Japanese student had copied long passages from a textbook. I was angry with that student and, generally speaking, I have little sympathy for those guilty of plagiarism. But I somehow felt that Hae-young's case was different. I called her to my office and explained the problem with her paper. Hae-young seemed genuinely surprised by what I had to say; though I cannot prove it, I was convinced that her bewilderment was real. She truly did not understand the American requirement that the language of a paper be her own, especially since she was largely just reporting on the research and opinions of others. She had time to go through one round of revisions before the end of the semester. The new version of the paper was still 50% acknowledged or unacknowledged quotations.

At this point, the deadline for final drafts was well passed, yet something led me to continue working with Hae-young. We met again, went through more revisions, then again, and then again. In all, Hae-young went through five or six versions of her paper, as our work together extended way beyond the end of the class; both of us seemed determined to get it right. In the end, Hae-young finally produced a paper that was, in my estimation, her work rather than a patchwork of the work of others; both of us breathed a sigh of relief.

The reason I tell this story now is to show what I mean by the contextually dependent nature of moral decision making in teaching. If I had acted according to the university regulations—which from a moral standpoint represent a way of treating all students equally—or if I had followed the ethical guidelines relating to plagiarism, I would not have given Hae-young an extra chance. I did what I did because from all that I could see, Hae-young's failure to write in the required manner was due not to laziness or a desire to deceive but to a genuine ignorance of U.S. academic expectations. (Pennycook [1996] has laid these issues out very clearly in an article published since the incident with Hae-young took place.) I made a moral decision to give her some leeway because I saw it as an educational opportunity, a chance for her to learn those expectations. For me, the educational value of leading Hae-young to this understanding outweighed the value of fairness in dealing with all students equally. In doing what I did, I had to accept that Hae-young could develop only from where she was and that to help her I had to practice what Noddings (1984) called *motivational displacement*: the ability "to see the other's reality as a possibility for my own" (p. 14). In this, I had to accept that the problem could not be fixed by merely rewriting but had to be reached organically by Hae-young herself—a process that took us far beyond the limits of the 15 weeks that the academy had laid out for learning to occur. I believe my decision was the right one; but it could be made only by taking into account all that I knew of Hae-young as a person and the nature of our educational relation in the class concerned, that is, the "uniqueness of human encounters." No abstract principle—for example, about how to handle plagiarism—could have led me to do what I did.

To return to the discussion about the nature of morality in teaching, the story of Hae-young brings me to a point I have already mentioned and that I think is illustrated in this story: In the decision-making processes of teaching, somewhere along the road rationality ceases to operate effectively. While many attempts at a rational morality have been made by philosophers (e.g., Gert, 1988, 1998), decisions and actions are motivated ultimately not by reason alone but also by beliefs held by individuals that cannot be based in or justified by reason alone. I call these kinds of belief *faith*, because they are based on a kind of trust we have in our own instincts, often bolstered by our personal experiences but rarely in the certainty that, for example, scientific knowledge can bring.

For instance, in my own teaching I am rather lax about deadlines: I rarely if ever penalize students for handing in written work late, so long as they let me know that they have to do so. I am not aware of any research literature that suggests that my practice (or the opposite, i.e., being strict about deadlines) has any influence one way or the other on students' learning. I do what I do because, for a variety of reasons, I *believe* it is the right thing to do. I believe that students' time and nervous energy are best spent producing a good paper rather than worrying about a usually artificial deadline, and I do not see my role as preparing teachers for expectations beyond the university (where deadlines are in many cases also routinely missed), but rather follow Dewey in seeing what we do in our own educational setting as being of value in itself and not merely a preparation for something else. However, I have no absolute authority to which I can turn to prove that the way I believe in is in fact the right and good way to deal with students. It may be that I am doing them a disservice by not being stricter. In fact, I think that it is impossible ever to know objectively whether I am right. I only have my own faith that I am doing the right thing.

This is the kind of educational belief I am talking about. In fact, much of what I (and, I think, others too) do as a teacher is grounded in certain beliefs that cannot be reached by reason. In this lie both the importance and the danger of acknowledging the centrality of morality in teaching: We recognize that our deepest and best instincts as teachers arise from belief or faith rather than from pure logic, yet by the same token we are deprived of the best tool we have for evaluating those instincts. This is a fundamental dilemma that informs all debate on morality in social settings such as teaching.

Furthermore, as my colleague Cary Buzzelli and I have pointed out (Buzzelli & Johnston, 2002), in educational contexts (as in others) morality has two other characteristics. First, it is highly complex: Even if we assumed that the morality of a particular individual is a reasonably straightforward thing (which it most certainly is not), in any given classroom the teacher is dealing not just with her own moral values but those of 20 or 30 other individuals, who are often themselves in the midst of moral growth and moral confusion. Second, in the overwhelming majority of cases it is run through with ambiguity. Teaching as an occupation involves constant rapid decision making. Many, if not most, of those decisions are moral in nature (e.g., the decision made by Peter, and the decisions I made with regard to Hae-young). However, these decisions are rarely if ever clear-cut; we rarely if ever have sufficient information to be completely sure of our decision, for the simple reason that no amount of information is ever enough. Indeed, in most morally ambiguous situations more information often clouds the issue even further. The simple decision of which students to devote one's special attention to is a moral decision, but it is also a moral dilemma. Spending time with a student is in most cases a good thing, yet to spend time with one student is not to spend it with others, and since the teacher's time, energy, and resources are always limited, the decision of which students need more attention is a moral one of determining whose need is the greatest and even how need is to be determined.

In this book, then, I interpret *morality* as the interplay between our personal, inner beliefs about what is right and wrong and good and bad (beliefs that are often, but not always, influenced by sociocultural values) and the social situations in which those beliefs play out. That is, morality is both individual (cognitive) and cultural (social) in nature. Furthermore, morality is deeply affected by context and at all times is both complex and ambiguous.

ETHICS, VALUES, AND IDEOLOGY

If *morality* is a difficult term, then *values* is even more problematic. One leading moral philosopher wrote bluntly: "I find it difficult to find a philosophical use for the noun 'value' that is not more clearly served by the words 'good,' 'bad,' 'harm' and 'benefit' and related terms like 'better' and 'worse'" (Gert, 1998, p. 94). Gert (1998) went on to acknowledge that the word is widely used but claimed that he does not understand these uses. However, as a nonphilosopher I am less confused by everyday uses of the term, or by its use, for example, in Julian Edge's (1996a) article entitled "Cross-Cultural Paradoxes in a Profession of Values," to which I refer more than once in this book. However, I believe that what Edge (1996a) referred to is the same thing that I call the *morality of teaching*; and, more generally speaking, I take the term *values* to refer to beliefs about what is right and good—the same meaning I have assigned to *morality*. This is close to the kinds of definitions used in research on values in education (Stephenson, Ling, Burman, & Cooper, 1998): for example, that values are "those beliefs held by individuals to which they attach special priority or worth, and by which they tend to order their lives" (Hill, 1991, cited in Ling & Stephenson, 1998, p. 3). Thus, in this book I use *morality* and *values* interchangeably, using the latter not just for stylistic variety but also to make connections with work such as Edge's and research in general education.

I also wish to clarify one distinction: that between morality and ethics. For philosophers, these two terms are generally interchangeable; *morality* is the subject of the branch of philosophy known as *ethics*. However, in professions such as teaching and research, the term *ethics* has taken on a more specific meaning: It refers to codified standards and rules governing professional practice. In this understanding, the difference between morality and ethics is that

> Ethical values may be imposed on members of a profession (such as teaching) by the collective in the form of professional organizations and governmental bodies. Examples include the mandating of confidentiality in reporting grades, or rules governing physical punishment. Morality, on the other hand, though it is usually played out in the social arena, also crucially involves personal, private values and beliefs. Thus, while it plays a central role in social activities such as teaching, it cannot be regulated by external institutions, but must always be mediated by individuals. (Buzzelli & Johnston, 2002, p. 5)

In this book I use the noun *ethics* and the adjective *ethical* only to refer to codes of behavior of this kind, although in quotations from other writers the word *ethics* may refer to what I call *morality*.

Last, I wish to say a word about ideology. I am in complete agreement with Gee (1990), who chided us for using the word *ideology* as if it were a biased set of values that other people might have but from which we ourselves are free. Like Gee, I believe that we all have ideologies and use them in our dealings with others. For me, *ideology* means nothing more or less than morality in political contexts; that is how I use the word in this book.

APPROACHES TO UNDERSTANDING MORALITY

Limitations of Philosophy

There is, of course, a vast literature on morality in the field of philosophy. Indeed, as I mentioned earlier, ethics, the study of morality, constitutes one of the primary domains of philosophical inquiry. As Rachels (1998) pointed out, philosophers have been drawn above all to address two overarching questions in this area. First, "are there objective truths" (p. 1), or is morality based only on our "feelings and social conventions" (p. 1)? Second, "how should we live, and why?" (p. 1)—in other words, what is the right way to lead one's life?

At certain points in this book I draw on some of the answers to these questions that different philosophers have proposed. Generally speaking, though, I have not found the philosophical literature to be very helpful in my goal of seeking to understand the moral foundations of language teaching. Part of the problem lies in the fact that the application of reason to such matters—the usual tool of philosophers—only takes us part of the way (Eisenberg, 1992). As I explained earlier, whether we like it or not, reason is of only limited use in considering how to teach, and likewise only some part of the teacher–student relation can be understood with reference to reason alone.

In addition, the discussions in the philosophical literature are usually of an abstract nature; where concrete examples are given, these are usually simplistic inventions, designed to point up the central issues of a moral problem rather than to explore the morality of everyday life. Let me take the first two examples that come to hand. In describing and analyzing an approach to moral values called *absolutism*, Wilson (1988) suggested the example of a person being absolutely opposed to torture and wrote: "Imagine … a case in which some tyrannical scientist is about to blow up the world […] we are to suppose that only by his being tortured will he reveal some secret which alone will prevent this" (p. 39). Another example, from Oderberg (2000), is: "Suppose Donald threatens to shoot Fred if he does not rape Celia" (p. 31). These situations do indeed present moral dilemmas, yet they are also extreme and very unlikely scenarios and ones which are distant from my own daily experiences—and, I hope, those of my readers. Our own experiences are also rich in moral dilemmas, but they seem to me to be of a different kind than these simplistic conundrums, which unfortunately dominate the literature of moral philosophy; this literature, however, does not include examples of problems I can recognize as belonging to my own life and those of my colleagues.

At the same time, it is undeniable that many of the ideas from the philosophical literature on morality have found their way into the collective subconscious. This is certainly true of utilitarianism, the philosophical approach to morality put forward initially by Bentham (1789/1948) and Mill (1863/1998) that claims that "the criterion of the rightness and wrongness of actions is whether they maximize good consequences" (Oderberg, 2000, p. 66), leading to the well-known motto of "the greatest happiness of the greatest number" (Rachels, 1998, p. 18). Such a principle can be seen, for instance, in the issue mentioned earlier of the way a teacher chooses to divide her time in attending to the competing needs of different learners. Thus, in some cases philosophical approaches will help us to make sense of our own unconscious assumptions and inclinations.

Furthermore, while philosophy may not aid us in solving our moral dilemmas, it can certainly help us to pose interesting questions. It seems to me that it is vital we ask ourselves: What is the right way to live? In our occupation, this question becomes: What is the right way to teach? Also, given the failure of science and methodology to provide comprehensive and convincing answers, our response to this question has to be moral in nature. Philosophy also leads us to ask: Are human beings fundamentally good, fundamentally bad, or fundamentally amoral? This may seem a high-blown question, but our answer will affect our actions as teachers in many domains—that of testing and evaluation, for example, where our view of human nature affects the degree of *trust* we evince in our assessment procedures (see chapter 4).

Finally, is there a universal human morality that transcends the moral values of particular cultures? This last question continues to bedevil philosophers and others (Harman & Thomson, 1996; Power & Lapsley, 1992), yet it would seem to be an issue in which we language teachers have both a stake and a say. If we believe in the existence of such an absolute morality, what does it consist of? How does it relate to national, cultural, or religious moralities? On the one hand, the creation of charters such as the *Universal Declaration of Human Rights* (1948), including a universal right to education (Spring, 2000), would seem to indicate that there is a set of values we humans all hold dear. On the other hand, the signal failure of pretty much every society on earth (however big or small) to honor these rights in full should give us pause for thought.

These are big, big questions yet, as I hope to show, our responses to them have very tangible consequences in the real world of our classrooms.

Noddings and Bauman

The most serious limitation of philosophy in terms of this book arises from its goal, which is different from my own. The goal of philosophy is usually to extract general truths from reflections on life, whereas my own purpose is to seek to understand specific moral situations and dilemmas. Even more than a practical philosophy, what I really need might be termed a *philosophy of practice*. The most useful approach of this kind is to be found in the work of educational philosopher Nel Noddings. Second, for my own purposes I need an approach that moves away from the generalities of traditional philosophical schemes and takes into consideration the agency of individuals, especially in a postmodern world in which overarching philosophical programs are a thing of the past and in which cultural and individual values are likely to come into conflict. Such an approach is offered by philosopher and social scientist Zygmunt Bauman.

Nel Noddings' (1984) book *Caring*, subtitled *A Feminine Approach to Ethics and Moral Education*, has been one of the most important influences on my own thinking. Noddings sees morality as inhering not within individuals but in the relation between them. She examines the nature of what she calls the "caring relation," the moral relation rooted in the "human affective response" (p. 3). Noddings takes relation as "ontologically basic" (p. 3), that is, "human encounter and affective response" are "a basic fact of human existence" (p. 4). She sees the caring relation as comprising an essentially unequal pair of the "one-caring" and the "cared-for" (p. 4), a relationship instantiated both by the mother–child relation and the teacher–student relation. In her book she explores the fundamental question of "how to meet the other morally" (p. 4).

Many aspects of Noddings' work appeal to me. She recognizes the morally colored nature of human relations while also acknowledging that in our efforts to do the right and good thing, "we shall not have absolute principles to guide us" (p. 5). In fact, she rejects the idea of ethical (i.e., what I call *moral)* principles and rules as "ambiguous and unstable" things that "separate us from each other" (p. 5); rather, she seeks to recognize and "preserve the uniqueness of human encounters": "Since so much depends on the subjective experience of those involved in ethical encounters, conditions are rarely 'sufficiently similar' for me to declare that you must do what I must do" (p. 5). Yet, in order to escape relativism, she maintains that the caring attitude is "universally accessible" (p. 5). Finally, her account of the caring relation is what she describes as "an essay in practical ethics" (p. 3), and I personally have found her conceptualization of the caring relation, in all its complexity, to be of more practical help in approaching the moral issues of my own profession than anything else I have found in the literature of moral philosophy.

A second writer, on whom I draw somewhat less, has also been a strong influence. In a series of books and articles, Zygmunt Bauman (e.g., 1993, 1994, 1995) has considered what has happened and may happen to morality in the postmodern age—an age in which the "grand narratives" and overarching moral and philosophical schemes have all been called into question, and the world "has lost its apparent unity and continuity" (Bauman, 1994, p. 16). Interestingly enough, Bauman believes that the end of the moral certainties offered by institutionalized moralities such as those of religion and politics does not mean the end of morality but instead is a liberating development that serves to "reinvigorate moral responsibilities" (p. 40) and allows us the freedom to reach for our own inner, personal morality while fundamentally rethinking the role of values in the public sphere. I find in Bauman's work strong support both for my own belief that ELT is a postmodern occupation *par excellence* (B. Johnston, 1999a, 1999b; see also Hargreaves, 1994) and for my continuing belief in humankind's fundamental moral sense.

TEACHING AS A MORAL ACTIVITY: FINDINGS FROM GENERAL EDUCATION

The moral dimension of teaching has long been recognized in general education. The education of children often involves conscious, explicit attention to inculcating particular values and character traits, but there is also a sense in which teachers unconsciously act as moral agents. Dewey (1909) was one of the first to draw attention to this aspect of morality in education; he distinguished between what is often referred to as "the teaching of morality"—explicit moral instruction—and "the morality of teaching"—the ways in which what teachers do in classrooms has inherent moral significance in itself. It is very much this latter meaning of morality with which I am concerned in this book.

In recent years, both theoretical and empirical research has explored the morality of teaching. Writers such as Tom (1984) and Noddings (1984, 1992) have developed a philosophy of education in which the teacher's role as moral agent is placed at center stage. Investigations of empirical data, on the other hand, have explored the ways in which moral issues and moral agency play out in classrooms and schools (Buzzelli & Johnston, 2002; Jackson, Boostrom, & Hansen, 1993; Noblit & Dempsey, 1996). I have much more to say about this literature, especially the theoretical framework proposed by Jackson et al. (1993), in chapter 2, in which I look at the moral substrate of classroom interaction in ELT.

There is in fact a large and growing empirical and theoretical literature of the moral in teaching. One may summarize its main findings and ideas as follows, while bearing in mind that all of these authors agree on one thing: Teaching is always and inevitably a profoundly value-laden undertaking, and one whose moral foundations are complex and deserve to be continually reflected on.

First, following Dewey's (1909) seminal work, teaching itself is seen as involving moral action (Tom, 1984). Teachers are moral agents (Bergem, 1990; Johnston, Juhász, Marken, & Ruiz, 1998), and education as a whole, and classroom interaction in particular, is fundamentally and inevitably moral in nature (D. L. Ball & Wilson, 1996; Goodlad, Soder, & Sirotnik, 1990). From the teacher's point of view, teaching involves constant and complex moral decision making (Tippins, Tobin, & Hook, 1993), and also a sensitivity to possibilities in contexts and individuals that Simpson and Garrison (1995) called *moral perception.*

Second, it is widely recognized that the ways in which values and moral issues are realized in the classroom are complex, subtle, and all pervasive. What Jackson et al. (1993) refer to as the *expressive morality* of the classroom includes what teachers and students say and how they behave but extends to every aspect of the situation, even the layout and decor of the classroom (see also B. Johnston & Buzzelli, 2002). The moral layeredness of classroom teaching (Hansen, 1993) must thus be acknowledged as a constant feature of educational contexts.

Third, there will always exist discrepancies among the various moral values played out in the classroom. These discrepancies may be seen as conflicts (Colnerud, 1997; Joseph & Ephron, 1993), moral dilemmas (D. K. Johnston, 1991), or as contradictions of values (Placier, 1996; Whitehead, 1993), or in terms of moral relativity (Willett, Solsken, & Wilson-Keenan, 1998), but in any case the notion of a single set of moral values for the classroom is highly problematic (Applebaum, 1996). A degree of uncertainty and ambiguity must always accompany discussion and analysis of the moral in classrooms and in education.

Last, there is also an ongoing debate in the area of moral education—an area that increasingly is seen as including the morality of teaching as well as the teaching of morality—between two opposing positions. One is that of *care,* as explicated in the work of Noddings and others. The other is the perspective of *justice,* based indirectly on the work of philosopher John Rawls (1971), in which equity—for example, equal attention to and equal opportunities for every child—is seen as the central principle. Although attempts have been made to resolve this apparent opposition (e.g., M. S. Katz, Noddings, & Strike, 1999), the very opposition itself presents a series of tough moral dilemmas.

VALUES IN ELT

My principal motivation for writing this book is the fact that, though many teachers I have spoken with acknowledge the profoundly moral nature of teaching, it has hardly ever been discussed in the professional literature of

ELT. Rather, language learning has almost exclusively been treated as a matter of psycholinguistic acquisition, while language teaching is a matter of techniques, activities, and methods. Although recent changes in these approaches—for example, recognizing the sociopolitical dimension of language learning (see chap. 3) and the fact that language teaching is a much more individual, complex, and idiosyncratic process than the notion of "method" allows (Kumaravadivelu, 1994; Prabhu, 1990)—have made our understanding of our work richer and fuller, these developments still have not explicitly addressed the values underlying much of what we do and the morality that I believe inheres in our work as teachers. This book, then, articulates a view of ELT that sees it as fundamentally and primarily moral in nature.

Though very little literature has addressed the morality of ELT in so many words, there have been the beginnings of such a discussion. This has mostly been couched in terms of ethics: the ethics of research (DuFon, 1993), of writing (Silva, 1997), and of testing (Hamp-Lyons, 1998; Shohamy, 1998), for example; see also Hafernik, Messerschmitt, and Vandrick's (2002) exploration of ethical issues in ESL teaching generally in the light of social justice concerns. While this literature represents a step in the right direction, I believe that the use of the term *ethics* also leads us astray somewhat. Certainly writers have associated it with the conception of ethics mentioned earlier: that of a code of professional practice rather than anything relating directly to moral beliefs and values. The discussion still lacks a direct engagement with beliefs about what is good and right.

To my knowledge, other than my own research (e.g., B. Johnston et al. 1998; B. Johnston, Ruiz, & Juhász, 2002) which I discuss in chapter 2, the only piece of writing in the field that addresses this topic directly and in detail is Edge's (1996a) article mentioned earlier, a written version of a plenary address Edge gave at the 1995 TESOL convention. In this article, which has been one of the most important and influential in my own professional development over the last few years, Edge (1996a) presented what he called three *paradoxes* (and what I might label *moral dilemmas*) of the field of TESOL. These are as follows:

- *Paradox 1: Sociopolitical context*—the clash between what Edge called *TESOL culture* and the inimical values of the broader national educational cultures in which it is situated.
- *Paradox 2: Liberation and domination*—the paradox that "to be involved in TESOL anywhere is to be involved in issues of liberation and domination everywhere" (p. 17).

- *Paradox 3: Foundations and fundamentalism*—the clash between the "respect for the right to be different" (p. 21) that our profession embraces and the intolerance that is sometimes a part of the views of our students that we have committed to respect.

In many ways, this article of Edge's is the starting point for my own analyses in this book (chap. 3, e.g., constitutes an exploration of Paradox 2). I thank Edge unreservedly for giving me direction. Edge prefers the word *values* to morality; but the spirit of his (1996a) article is very much consonant with my thesis in this book, and I feel he would agree with me that *values* and *morality* refer to the same thing. What he writes supports the idea, confirmed by many, many teachers I have worked with and spoken to, that ELT teaching is indeed a profoundly moral undertaking.

First, all that I wrote in the previous section about the moral dimensions of teaching in general education applies to language teaching. Like any form of teaching, ELT crucially involves relations between people, and relations, as explained earlier, are fundamentally moral in character: The intimate relationship among who we are, how others see us, and how we treat and are treated by those others, is above all a question of human values. Second, ELT involves efforts to change people; we assume that such change is meant to be for the better, and thus it is a moral endeavor. Last, as with any kind of teaching, our actions as teachers can only ever partially be derived from "objective" or "scientific" principles: What science (in our case, e.g., the scientific study of second language acquisition) can tell us is inadequate; it is of only limited help in the design of materials and none whatsoever in matters such as how to deal with unruly students, administrations who impose books and syllabi on us, or classrooms with furniture bolted to the floor. In all these matters and many more, the courses of action we choose as teachers cannot be based in scientific knowledge but must spring from a sense that the materials we select for our students and the ways we interact with them are right and good.

Although second language teaching is in many other ways like all other teaching, the morality of this form of teaching also has certain qualities unique to our field. For example, to an extent not usually experienced in general education (or at least not acknowledged in its literature), values in second language teaching are virtually by definition negotiated across cultural boundaries. Given the centrality of values in culture, this fact becomes a huge influence on the moral contours of the classroom.

Second, profound ambiguities attend this cross-cultural meeting of values in various contexts. Though these ambiguities are present in all language teaching, they are often particularly salient in English language teaching in both ESL and EFL contexts. In EFL, we are faced with the problem of presenting, explaining, and, in many cases, justifying cultural practices that we ourselves often believe to be either superior or inferior to those of the students' culture. Native speakers become unwitting representatives for their own "national culture" as perceived by others (Duff & Uchida, 1997; B, Johnston, 1999a). In other cases they are called on to fulfill roles that run counter to their own culture: An American colleague of mine who taught in a Japanese middle school, for example, found himself constantly wrestling with the expectation in Japan that schoolteachers intervene consciously and overtly in the moral lives of the children—for example, upbraiding the children for transgressions of behavior in ways that in the United States are reserved for the parents of the children concerned (see also Hadley & Evans, 2001). Non-native speakers, on the other hand, who constitute the great majority of the world's teachers of English, find themselves called on to act as representatives of the cultures they teach. In ESL we have the problem of balancing respect for the home cultures with our responsibility as teachers to facilitate integration into the new cultural environment (I present an example of a moral dilemma arising from this problem shortly).

Third, for many of us who work primarily with adults, there is the additional fact that our learners should not be treated as if they need to be overtly educated in moral matters but should be assumed to be in charge of their own moral development. The overt moral instruction that accompanies the teaching of children is absent. At the same time, for immigrant and refugee learners in particular we may believe that they *do* need to learn different values. Let me share with you an example of this dilemma:

I once spoke with an adult literacy tutor in a small Indiana town who found herself having to explain to one of her Russian students that in America one is expected to wear a clean shirt to work each day and not to wear the same shirt 2 or more days running. While this is, objectively speaking, true about "American culture," it also constitutes an infringement of another basic American rule: that one does not comment on the personal hygiene and habits of other adults. The teacher found that she felt morally obligated to transgress this second law in the interests of supporting her student's success and acceptance in the new environment.

I find this example particularly telling because it reveals not just the moral underpinnings of ELT but also the complex and ambiguous nature of those underpinnings. In this case, the teacher's moral duty to do well by her students as students is balanced by her moral duty to treat them with respect as human equals; the infantilism always lurking beneath the surface of adult ELT is all the more problematic because while in an abstract, humanistic sense our learners are fully fledged adults, in many practical ways—especially their command of the language and their grasp of cultural norms of the target culture—they do in fact resemble children.[3] (In chap. 5 I look at another example of the moral complexities of teachers "interfering" in the personal lives of students.)

Last, the very nature of the language teaching profession is often significantly different from that of general education. Unlike many occupations, it is international virtually by definition and thus cannot comfortably rest its morality on conventional national cultural models (even setting aside the problematic nature of such models). In addition, although a lot of English teaching goes on in national educational systems, an exceptionally large percentage is conducted outside of primary and secondary public education: In private schools, in university programs that themselves are marginalized, in community programs, and so on. Many teachers (myself included) do not hold a teaching qualification recognized by the state, and for all teachers, including those in public K–12 education, the knowledge base of English language teaching is fundamentally different from that of content subjects such as history or chemistry. Whereas in these subjects a major part of knowledge involves knowing facts, knowing a language primarily involves a skill—it is a process-centered knowledge base. In many contexts this sets teachers apart from their colleagues, for they are often judged not so much on the basis of their specialized knowledge (and much less their teaching ability) but on their own skill in using the language. All these things set ELT and its teachers apart from general education. This fact, too, has a significant impact on the moral dimension of language teaching.

Such factors, then, lend the moral dimension of language teaching a particular character, one that colors our work and our moral analysis of it in highly complex and polyvalent—that is, multi-valued—ways.

Though this complexity and polyvalence cannot be avoided or ignored, it does matter what position one takes on moral matters. I wish to make my own position clear. I believe firmly in the dignity of all learners, and in the need to support the empowerment of learners both inside and outside class. Like many teachers, I found myself drawn to this occupation

---

[3]I realize that this is an unpopular position to take, yet I believe it does reflect the truth. It certainly captures my own experience—I have frequently felt like a child in radically different cultural settings. However, I wish to emphasize that this view of students in no way justifies infantilism in classroom methodology or materials. I believe very firmly that adult students must at all times be treated as adults. Our difficulty as teachers—another moral dilemma that we face—is finding ways to do this with students whose linguistic proficiency runs so far behind their intellectual abilities.

because I find it fascinating and invigorating to work with people from different cultures, and I feel a moral duty to be their advocate. However, I also feel a moral duty to acknowledge and face up to the ambiguity and polyvalence of what we do—in other words, that blithely accepting "empowerment," for example, as an uncomplicated and unalloyed good serves neither our own cause nor the interests of our students. It is only by confronting the moral complexity and ambiguity of our teaching that we can hope to identify the good and right things to do in any given set of circumstances, that is, to know the right way to teach.

QUESTIONS FOR REFLECTION AND DISCUSSION

1. Consider the three stories I tell in this chapter: Peter's story about the Palestinian student, my story about Hae-young, and the adult literacy teacher's story about the Russian student. In each of these stories, the teacher could have taken a different decision. What other options were available? How do you think you would have handled the situation? Most interestingly, what values or moral beliefs would have led you to your decision?

2. Peter's story ends with the teacher giving a student a grade different from the one the student really deserves. Have you ever given a student a grade different to the grade he or she really deserved based on performance in class? Why did you do what you did? What values or moral reasons were behind your decision? If the same situation occurred today, would you do the same thing?

3. Have you ever had a case of plagiarism in your class? How did you handle it? What factors about the context—the student concerned, the nature of the plagiarism, the stakes involved—played a part in deciding what you should do?

4. Have you ever made comments on a student's physical appearance, way of dressing, or personal hygiene? In the context in which you teach, to what extent are such comments expected or frowned on? Do you agree with these expectations?

5. What values inform your own teaching? Where do these values come from? To what extent do you feel that your values agree with widely accepted national, cultural, religious, or political norms? To what extent do you feel that your own personal values run counter to these norms?

6. Think of one incident in your teaching in which you had to make a decision that involved conflicts of values such as those described in this chapter. If you are working with others, first tell the story of this incident. What conflicting values were at stake? How did you resolve the dilemma? What values led you to the decision you made?

2

Morality in Classroom Interaction

I begin this chapter in the place best known to teachers and where many of us feel most comfortable: the classroom. My claim in this book is that all aspects of teaching are value laden, and it seems to me that if what I say is to have any validity, I must first and foremost show how values and moral dilemmas are played out in the minute-to-minute business of classroom teaching. At this point I also wish to make two foundational points. First, I want to emphasize that, while there are better and worse courses of action that teachers can take in particular circumstances—that is, that their decisions matter—these decisions are always complex and polyvalent. Thus, as I consider the moral meanings inherent in the things teachers say and do in classrooms I wish to underline the fact that I am not standing in judgment over the teachers concerned but merely trying to understand the values underlying their actions and decisions. Second, one of the reasons for the moral complexity of classroom interaction is that it is not only the moral agency of the teacher that is at play but also the moral agency of each learner. In this chapter, as in the book as a whole, I focus primarily on the teacher, because this is my main topic of interest; however I acknowledge that in all contexts, the students are active and equally important participants in the teacher–student relation.

To best illustrate the complexities and intricacies of the moral dimensions of classroom interaction, I focus on three aspects of interaction in English language classrooms: the moral dimensions of classroom discourse, values implicit in curricula, and the moral underpinnings and moral consequences of the teacher's de facto role as representative of an institution.

THE MORAL DIMENSIONS OF LANGUAGE CLASSROOM DISCOURSE

Searching for the Moral in Classroom Discourse

In this section I share some data from a study my colleagues and I conducted in an Intensive English Program (IEP) at a midwestern university in the United States. (Johnston, Juhász, Marken, & Ruiz, 1998). In this study we examined transcripts from the classes of three ESL teachers for moments of moral significance.

I mentioned above that in English language teaching (ELT) very little empirical research has been published looking at the moral dimensions of classroom discourse. In fact, to the best of my knowledge the study I will describe here was the first of its kind. However, my colleagues and I were very fortunate to have access to comparable work in general education. We were particularly influenced by a book by Philip Jackson, Robert Boostrom, and David Hansen (1993) entitled *The Moral Life of Schools*. This book describes the results of a 2.5-year study involving intensive observation and analysis of classroom interaction in a variety of public and private schools and focusing on the teacher's role as moral agent. On the basis of their observations and analysis, Jackson et al. proposed eight "categories of moral influence" (p. 2), which fall into two sets. The first set involves overt reference to moral principles, of the kind associated with the "teaching of morality": teachers exhorting children to behave in particular ways, posters with motivational slogans, and so on. The second set of categories of moral influence, on the other hand, constitute the "morality of teaching"; they are the ways in which the processes of education in general, and the actions of teachers in particular, send subtle, implicit moral messages in and of themselves. Jackson et al. proposed three such categories: (a) classroom rules and regulations, (b) the curricular substructure, and (c) expressive morality (pp. 11–42).

The *rules and regulations* "deemed to be essential for the conduct and well-being of the [class]room's inhabitants" (p. 12) include rules of conduct such as how to ask questions or participate in classroom events. Jackson et al. (1993) suggested that such rules come close "to constituting an explicit moral code that all of the students in the room are expected to obey" (p. 12).

The *curricular substructure* comprises "conditions that operate to sustain and facilitate every teaching session in every school in every subject within the curriculum" (Jackson et al., 1993, pp. 15–16). These conditions thus underlie the form and content of curricula in different subjects. According to Jackson et al. (1993), these conditions have two outstanding qualities: they are "seldom explicitly acknowledged by either teachers or students" (p. 16), and they are imbued with moral meaning. The curricular substructure can be thought of as "enabling conditions" (p. 16). Jackson et al. described them as "an elaborate amalgam of shared understandings, beliefs, assumptions, and presuppositions, all of which enable the participants in a teaching situation to interact amicably with each other and work together, thus freeing them to concentrate on the task at hand" (p. 16). They include the *assumption of truthfulness*—that what teachers and students say in class is true—and the *assumption of worthwhileness*—that there is inherent value in the topics and materials covered in class.

Expressive morality describes the often extremely subtle ways in which moral judgments about what is good and bad, right and wrong, are conveyed in the classroom. Expressive morality resides not just in the words teachers use but also in their tone of voice, in their facial expressions and gestures, and in elements such as the arrangement of chairs in the classroom or the decor on the walls. Jackson et al. (1993) wrote of "vaporlike emanations of character" (p. 34) that carry moral meaning and described moral judgments as being "embedded" (p. 35) in actions and objects. The act of analysis consists of a sensitization to the particular moral meanings inherent in these emanations.

Because this set of categories emerged from long and careful observation of classrooms, we decided that it would provide a very useful way of framing our own study. Thus, we used this set of three categories of moral influence as our conceptual framework. In the rest of this section I share some examples of classroom data illustrating each of the categories and discuss the moral meanings that we found to be encoded in the discourse.

Classroom Rules and Regulations

The IEP in which our research took place had an enrollment of about 300–400 students at the time of the study. It offered classes in general English but with an emphasis on preparation for higher education. Most IEP classes were small (10–15 students). One class, however, known as the "mini-course," had a much higher enrollment and was a content-based class intended to offer students the experience of a larger lecture course to prepare them for what they might experience on enrollment in regular university classes.

In the session in question the teacher of the mini-course was Joe, a doctoral student with several years' teaching experience. Joe had taught the same class in the previous session and had had significant problems with attendance, among other things, which was very difficult to check in a class of 50 or more students. This led Joe to devise a scheme whereby each student was assigned to a numbered seat in the large lecture hall where the class was held; this system made it much easier to be able to check quickly who was present. On the first day of the new class, Joe presented his syllabus. Part of the syllabus read as follows, in bold print:

ATTENDANCE:

Your participation is essential for this course. Student input will be of particular importance and your attendance will be vital to your success in the course. THERE ARE NO EXCUSED ABSENCES UNLESS APPROVED BY THE INSTRUCTOR OR THE IEP PROGRAM. IF YOU ARE ABSENT MORE THAN *10* TIMES FOR THIS CLASS, YOU WILL BE GIVEN A "U" FOR THE COURSE. Each student will be assigned a seat in the classroom and he/she must sit in the given seat for attendance. If the student is not in his/her seat, he/she will be marked absent and given a "U" for participation.

Tardiness:

Please do not be late for class.

If you are more than 10 minutes late to class, you will be considered absent. (B. Johnston et al., 1998, p. 168)

From the point of view of values and morality, a number of interesting observations can be made about this passage. Perhaps most striking is its tone, which sets particular expectations for the teacher–student relation, more or less defining it as a matter of power relations between them and not only ignoring but counteracting the less confrontational, more supportive caring relation envisioned by Noddings (1984; see chap. 1). Second, it presupposes a lack of trust on behalf of the teacher, an issue I discuss in more detail in chapter 4. The lack of trust, moreover, arises from the fact that this group of learners, whom the teacher has never met before, are being prejudged on the basis of a previous, different group of learners—another denial of the unique relation between teacher and student. Last, and also impinging on the teacher–student relation, students are identified only by their seat number; thus, a further dehumanizing of the students seems to be taking place.

On the other hand, it is vital not to leap to premature condemnation of Joe or his methods. Joe was attempting to minimize class time spent on checking attendance—a program requirement—and thus maximize student engagement with the material. Furthermore, few teachers would disagree with the idea that attendance in class is highly desirable, and, in language learning, often essential, or with the suggestion that, much as we might have general respect for the freedom and agency of others, without some form of coercion certain students will simply not do what they are supposed to and what it is in their best interests to do. Last, I want to stress that Joe is not one of nature's authoritarians; he is a warm and caring teacher whose strictness in this syllabus was occasioned by real problems encountered in the previous session. Indeed, as we reported in the study (B. Johnston et al., 1998), immediately after going over this part of the syllabus in class, Joe apologized to the class for its severe tone, sensing its dissonance with his own internal notion of the teacher–student relation. He explained this dissonance in a journal entry:

> This apology was one of those "moments" when the instructor senses hidden dimensions underlying classroom speech acts. At the time of my apology, I seemed compelled to rebel against the very rules I had established as a part of the classroom discourse. […] At the instant of the apology, I attempted to take a milder tone for fear of breaking a bond between myself and the class. In other words, the discourse of communication was clashing with the discourse of classroom rules. (B. Johnston et al., p. 170)

The conflicting messages being sent in this case exemplify the terribly complex moral dilemmas that underlie the enactment of rules and regulations, that is, the exercise of power and authority in the classroom. Much as we may condemn authoritarian approaches such as that exemplified in Joe's seating arrangement, in many cases such actions arise from entirely understandable moral reasoning. In this case, Joe wished to create the conditions for the best possible learning and teaching to take place in his class; to this end, however, he found that he needed to exercise a firm hand—so firm, in fact, that it went against other values he held deeply (the "bond" between teacher and student that he wrote about). More generally, we can say that the exercise of power constitutes moral action, yet the values encoded in particular acts of power and authority are complex and contradictory and are open to multiple and conflicting understandings.

The Curricular Substructure of ESL

Damon, another teacher whose classroom we studied, had taught in Japan for some years before taking a position in the IEP while he completed his master's degree in the United States. Damon was teaching a low-intermediate reading class. In one class, Damon was leading his students through a general-knowledge quiz about what to do in particular driving situations.

Teacher: OK, so the first one: [*reads from the book*] "Every time you turn on your windshield wipers you should also turn on your headlights." What do you think? True or false?

Student 1: False.

Teacher: False? Anybody else? M. says false. Tell me what *you* think. Tell me what *you* think. OK? P. says false. Only two of you are going to answer? Tell me what you think. I don't care. You can be wrong. Or you can be right. Or it doesn't matter. When it rains, do y— ah, let me ask you this: when it rains, do you turn on your headlights?

Student 2: Yeah.

Teacher: Yeah?

Student 2: Yeah.

Student 3: Sure.

[…]

[*Teacher and class work through the second question*]

Teacher: Next one. [*Reads from the book*] "If you think you're going to run head on into another vehicle, it is better to drive off the road than to crash." Right, so you're in a bad situation; you think you're going to run on, head on into someone or something; it's better to drive off the road than to crash. What do you think? True or false? Who thinks it—

Student 4: Highway?

Teacher: Yeah, drive off the highway, don't have the crash. It's better to drive off the highway? Who thinks it's true?

> One. Two. Three. Only three? Who thinks it's false?
> One.

[Students laugh]

Teacher: *[laughing]* You guys! Last one. You can, it doesn't matter, just say something.

(class of 4/1/96; B. Johnston et al., 1998, p. 173)

In this passage, Damon is struggling to get his students to respond to the items of the quiz. In analyzing the extract, my colleagues and I were particularly struck by the complex and contradictory moral messages encoded in what Damon says to his students. It seemed to us that the passage reveals a certain moral paradox at the heart of communicative language teaching regarding the nature and purpose of student participation.

One of the most basic underlying tenets of communicative language teaching is that language is not merely a set of forms (words, grammatical structures, etc.) but is used *for* something: to convey information, maintain relationships, and act in and on the social world (Finocchiaro & Brumfit, 1983; Halliday, 1978). In all of these ends, the substance of what is said is the important thing. In the context of Damon's class, this means that the students' opinion about the right answer is most important—more important, for example, than forming that opinion in a grammatically faultless way. Thus, Damon urges his students: "Tell me what *you* think. Tell me what *you* think." The message that the individual learner has to convey is paramount; in the language of communicative teaching, the classroom is *meaning centered* and *learner centered* (Finocchiaro & Brumfit, 1983; Nunan, 1988).

Yet there is also another side to this. Much communicative teaching involves games or relatively trivial topics—for many people, the driving quiz Damon is using might fit into the latter category. There is a sense that the content of the class is in fact *not* important and that it is simply engagement with the language that matters. Indeed, second language acquisition scholarship has shown that fluency can be achieved only by actually speaking and that it is important to maximize the time that each student has for production—hence the widespread use of pair work in communicative language teaching, which multiplies the opportunities each student has to produce the language (Brown, 1994). In light of this, it is pedagogically important to urge the students to produce as much language as possible. Damon does this by saying: "Just say anything," implying that it is the making of language that matters, not its content.

Yet these two values are incompatible. On the one hand, what learners have to say is the most important thing; on the other hand, it is irrelevant, and mere production is what matters. Yet both values stem from the same goal: to make the language learning process more effective.

This is the paradox that underlies Damon's struggle in the previous passage. At one level he is urging the students to make their contributions individual and meaning based: "Tell me what *you* think. Tell me what *you* think." The moral message implicit here is that he wants communication of ideas: that is, the teacher–student relation is paramount. Yet simultaneously he is sending the message that the most important thing is simply to practice fluency: "Just say something." Here, the moral subtext is that the students have a moral duty—based on the *assumption of participation*, another part of the curricular substructure—to participate, and that this participation is in fact in their best interests, because it is the most effective way for them to achieve their goal of learning English. The moral dilemma is captured when Damon says: "I don't care. You can be wrong. Or you can be right. Or it doesn't matter." The phrase "I don't care" in particular encapsulates the ambiguity: It can mean both "I will accept any answer" and yet also "I am indifferent to what you say," both of which meanings impinge on the teacher–student relation.

It is this paradox and this ambiguity that Damon is wrestling with in the extract quoted earlier; one could also argue that the same paradox contributes to his students' unwillingness to participate. In any case, the double meaning of *participation* in language classrooms is not Damon's problem alone but a complex and contradictory moral issue all of us face in our teaching. This is perhaps the most fundamental moral dilemma at the heart of the curricular substructure of the communicative classroom.

Expressive Morality in ESL Classrooms

The third teacher in our study, Jackie, also had several years' experience and had completed her master of arts degree a few years before we conducted the study. She was teaching an elective course for advanced students in which she focused on issues in American life through the medium of film. One of these issues was male–female roles and relationships. The class in question comprised a small group of Koreans and one Taiwanese; the class was all women except for two Korean men. The following extract was taken from a class discussion concerning working women.

Teacher: What about you? Will you work after you return [to Korea]?

Student 1
(female):   No, I don't know.

Teacher: Why? What will determine whether you work? Your husband?

Student 1: There's an idea that if a wife works, it shows a failure of the husband. Some kinds of jobs of the husband can support a wife.

Teacher: Guys? Do you want your wife to work?

Student 2
(male):   If she wants a job, I'll allow her to work.

Teacher: You'll *allow* her?

[*General laughter*]

Teacher: So how will you decide yes or no?

Student 2: [???]

Teacher: Would you like her to work? What kind of job? Business jobs?

Student 2: No, business is too hard and she would have to work too many hours.

(class of 4/16/96; B. Johnston et al.,1998, p. 176)

In this extract, what was of most interest to us was the matter of expressive morality, the subtle ways in which what the teacher does or says sends moral messages. Specifically, it seemed to us that powerful and complex messages were contained both in the clash of values the situation reveals and in Jackie's response to the male student: "You'll *allow* her?"

At first glance, the situation looks like one of the cross-cultural clashes of values that occur with some frequency in language teaching (Scollon & Wong Scollon, 1995). Yet there is more to this than meets the eye. The Korean male student's statement that he would allow his wife to work, though it seems initially to be a classic case of a patronizing attitude, can also be read differently: Given that he is in a position to *not* allow her, he chooses to let her find work—in other words, he is choosing to be liberal, within the Korean context, that is. Also, it seems that the students do not hold this belief blindly but can see it from the outside, as it were, from the perspective of an American such as Jackie—hence their laughter at her response.

Jackie's response to the student is also interesting. Jackie herself is a militant believer in the equality of the sexes; she is also an ESL teacher. In her response, she refrains from any explicit judgment of what the student said, and in so doing, she is adhering to the value of respect for students and their views which, I have argued at several points in this book, is one of the cornerstones of the ELT profession (Edge, 1996a; Teachers of English to Speakers of Other Languages, 2001). At the same time, however, another moral imperative—that of being true to one's own values, and of acting on the world in ways that one believes are right—leads Jackie to encode her view not in her words but in her stress and intonation: Her obviously ironic (though equally obviously restrained) echoing of the student places heavy stress on the word *allow* and a rising (questioning) intonation on the sentence as a whole. The students' laughter indicates that they have "got it"—that the moral judgment has come across loud and clear despite its being conveyed so obliquely. Yet the briefly quoted continuation of the extract, in which the students continue to discuss the matter, imply strongly that the other side of Jackie's message—her refusal to condemn explicitly, and her receptiveness to what the students have to say regardless of whether she supports it—has also been understood.

The great moral complexity of even such a short and simple passage reveals the rich and difficult nature of expressive morality. Even the slightest and subtlest things that we do or say in the classroom have moral significance and convey complicated and often contradictory moral messages. This process is not merely unavoidable but desirable, because it reinforces the fundamentally moral character of classroom teaching, and especially that of the teacher–student relation. While we cannot and should not avoid it, I would argue that it is in our interest to become aware of the moral meanings our words and actions may convey and to sensitize ourselves to this usually invisible but always important dimension of classroom interaction.

The Dilemma of Voice in Classrooms

The three categories of Jackson et al.'s (1993) framework that I have examined convey some of the richness and complexity of the moral dimensions of classroom interaction, but they by no means exhaust the possibilities for morally significant events and exchanges in classes. Many other areas of classroom discourse can be shown to have a moral substrate. As a single example, I look briefly at the moral dilemma of voice in the language classroom (Bailey & Nunan, 1996; Jaworski, 1992; McElroy-Johnson, 1993;

Tsui, 1996). As before, I ground this discussion in a piece of classroom data. This time the data come from a second study my colleagues and I conducted in the spring of 2000 (B. Johnston, Ruiz, & Juhász, 2002). In this study, we took a more detailed look at a single classroom, that of Mary, a highly experienced teacher and many-year veteran of the same IEP, whose upper intermediate class was entitled "Communication" and was primarily intended to provide opportunities for spoken practice. In the following extract, from the penultimate week of the 7-week session, Mary is negotiating with her students which topic from the book they would rather look at next: sleep, or abnormal psychology. It focuses on Young, a Korean student and the only woman in the group.

> Teacher: Can [Turkish name], I think is going with Abnormal-ity. [*Laughs; looks around and waits for answers or suggestions. Nobody says anything for a few seconds.*] Yasuo, which would you prefer to talk about, abnormal behavior or sleep?
>
> Yasuo: Abnormal behavior.
>
> Teacher: Abnormal behavior. Young? [*Young doesn't look up, avoiding eye contact; she looks at her book. There is silence for 12 seconds.*] If you had a choice, which would you talk about, sleep or abnormal behavior? [*Waits for 3 seconds; there is no answer from Young. She turns to the next student*] Diego?
>
> Diego: Sleep.
>
> Teacher: Sleep. Okay, you know where *you* stand. Marcio?
>
> (class of 2/17/00; B. Johnston, Ruiz, & Juhász, 2002)

Young was a shy and quiet Korean woman in a small group dominated by talkative men from countries such as Turkey, the United Arab Emirates, Brazil, and Argentina. In most of the classes we observed, Young managed to say something, but usually it seemed to be an effort for her. In this class, for whatever reason, she failed to respond to Mary's prompting and extended wait time, to the point where Mary moved on to the next student without a contribution from Young.

We can only speculate on the reasons for Young's silence at this time, and on her thoughts and feelings as she waited out what must have seemed a terribly long 12 seconds of silence in an otherwise noisy class.

These are important matters, too. However, since my focus in this chapter, as in the book in general, is on the teacher, I wish to consider for a moment the moral dilemma faced by Mary.

It seems to me that at this point in the class Mary is caught between two opposing sets of values regarding voice in the language classroom. On the one hand, there is respect for a student's right to be silent and for the very human difficulty of shyness; this, in turn, springs from our more general concern that each student feel comfortable and stress-free in class. Protecting students from stress is a general response aimed at the well-being of the student, coming from our care for the student in our role in the teacher–student relation; it is also a more purely educational value, since many teachers (myself included) believe that stress, at least too much of the wrong kind, is counterproductive—a belief expressed in Krashen's (1981) notion of the affective filter. Last, allowing the student to remain silent also conveys respect for the student's right to choose when she does or does not have something to say—that is, it acknowledges her agency and empowerment in the matter of voice.

On the other hand, however, powerful values move the teacher to do her utmost to get Young to say something. Balancing the student's right to silence is her right to voice: the right for her opinion to be heard and to count in the collective of the class. In this understanding, "silence" is a negative value, associated with the notion of "silencing" and "being silenced" (Delpit, 1995; McLaughlin & Tierney, 1993; Weis & Fine, 1993). In light of this value, Mary attempts to bring Young into the community of the class as a fully fledged member, with all the rights this brings, including the right to participate in the negotiation of the syllabus (Breen, 1984; Irujo, 2000). In addition, there is a good educational reason to encourage Young to speak: As mentioned earlier, we know from both research and our own experience that producing language significantly enhances acquisition—that, in the words of the Spanish proverb, "we make the road by walking."[1] For this reason too Mary encourages Young to speak.

I believe the dilemma just outlined underlies any attempt by a teacher to draw speech from reluctant students. No two students are alike; each brings a different level and kind of anxiety or shyness to class. Some students talk far too much, silencing others. Yet in each case, and at each

---

[1] The proverb appears in poem XXIX of a cycle entitled *Proverbios y cantares* (Proverbs and Songs) by the Spanish poet Antonio Machado y Ruiz (1875–1939). The poem contains the lines:

Caminante, no hay camino,
se hace camino al andar.

("Traveler, there is no road; The road is made by walking"; Machado, 1941, p. 212)

moment of the class, the teacher must weigh the competing values of voluntary silence versus enforced speech in deciding what is in the best interests of the learner concerned and the best interests of the other learners in the class. In each case, this will be a moral decision regarding what is good and right for the students.

Finding the Moral in Language Classrooms

As I mentioned earlier, the discussion here by no means exhausts the moral dimensions of classroom interaction. That has not been my intention. Rather, by showing the layers of moral meanings that can be discerned in even apparently unremarkable instances of classroom talk, I am suggesting that all aspects of classroom discourse are infused with moral significance. Furthermore, as I hope is clear from these examples, moral meanings cannot be simplistically mapped onto things that teachers and students say and do using some kind of rudimentary coding, but are crucially dependent on details of the specific teacher–student relations involved. Put another way, the same expression or action by different teachers with different students will carry very different moral meanings. Furthermore, whereas some words and actions are more morally desirable than others, it is also the case that all classroom discourse carries complex and conflicting values, and that much of what teachers are doing as they make decisions in the language classroom involves weighing up, usually rapidly and unconsciously, the values at play in particular circumstances in order to make their decisions. My message in this section has been that bringing this process to consciousness enhances the options we have as teachers in determining the good and right courses of action to follow in our teaching.

VALUES AND CURRICULUM IN ELT

Moral values are not only found in classroom interaction and in various aspects of the teacher–student relation; they also inhere in, and can be read from, the things that are studied in ELT classrooms across the world—what I refer to loosely as *curriculum*. In this section I examine three aspects of values in the ELT curriculum. First, I look at the moral meanings that can be found in a typical ELT textbook. Second, I consider the moral issues at play in determining which variety of English pronunciation is to be endorsed in the classroom. Last, I consider the moral dilemma that underlies the teaching of second language writing.

Values in the Textbook

Published materials are a major presence in ELT classrooms. First, teachers and students spend a lot of time with them. Second, in many places there is no formal written curriculum, and so materials such as course books constitute a de facto curriculum in themselves (Hutchinson & Torres, 1994; this, for example, was very definitely the case where I taught in Poland). Such materials, then, are a central component in classroom interaction. Furthermore, like everything else in classrooms, textbooks and other materials convey morally significant messages.

It is beyond the scope of this book to provide a detailed analysis of moral meanings in textbooks in general; rather, in line with my argument that all materials carry moral meanings, I have selected for examination here one book at random from the shelves of the small library of our IEP. The book is *Freeway: An Integrated Course in Communicative English*, written by Cheryl Pawlik and Anna Stumpfhauser de Hernandez (1995) and published by Longman; I chose Student Book 2 to examine. I selected this book merely as an example; the kinds of comments I make about it here could be made of any published textbook. I deliberately took the first book I found from the shelf and did not look at other books there (though of course I am familiar with many of them from my own teaching experiences and those of my students).

Even with just a single textbook (and, at 80 pages, a slim one at that), there is a vast array of issues that could be addressed. I focus on three things: the representation of American culture, the role of the learner, and content versus form.

On page 12 of the book there is a short article, accompanied by a picture, about a "sport" called "turkey bowling," which involves the player sliding a frozen turkey across the floor of a supermarket and trying to knock over 10 large plastic bottles of soda. The article gives the rules of turkey bowling and explains that it "is becoming a popular sport in California."

One question that occurs to me is: Should this kind of article be included? I ask this for a number of reasons. First, while some people might find this activity to be merely amusing and quirky, others will find it somewhat distasteful. Second, there is also a matter of representation (Buzzelli & Johnston, 2002; Harklau, 2000): What image of American society does this convey, and is that image accurate and fair? As someone who has lived in the United States for 11 years now, this activity strikes me as being rather an unusual one compared with the other ways in which Americans spend their time, yet it is the kind of thing that often finds its way into European newspapers (and perhaps others) and conveys the image of America as a land of the bizarre and the tacky. Do students understand this? Does it matter? At one level, I would definitely suggest that this is an improvement over generalized descriptions of "American culture" found in certain textbooks, yet on another level, it seems that its representation of American culture is questionable.

Returning to the matter of personal reactions to turkey bowling, it is also striking to me that the responses of students are nowhere envisioned in this unit. The only activity involves a cartoon of a man throwing a live turkey at some glass bottles and asks the students to find which rules of turkey bowling he is breaking. The unit then moves on to other topics. The fact that student response is ignored is of considerable moral significance and recalls my earlier discussion of voice. What students bring to the activity is irrelevant, as are their own reactions to what they read. In terms of the teacher–student relation, one side is silenced; there can be no relation through these kinds of materials. My guess is that many teachers would choose to add an activity or at least a discussion asking the students for their responses to the text, precisely to recapture the human dimension of the teacher–student relation; but nothing like this is included in the materials themselves.

The reason for this omission can be seen in the title of this unit. It is headed: "Have To/Don't Have To." Other units are called "Personal Descriptions," "Past Tense of 'To Be,'" "Object Pronouns/Making a Telephone Call," and so on. In other words, the book is arranged primarily according to grammatical structures and linguistic functions, which provide the coherence within each unit; this means that substantive topics shift within the units. The passage on turkey bowling is followed by an activity that asks "Make a list of things that students in your school have to and don't have to do"; then there is a listening passage on another sport; then students are asked to make parallel sentences about another sport; then to talk in pairs about their responsibilities at home; and so on, all within the space of two pages. There is little or no thematic coherence here or elsewhere in the book.

This fact reflects a dilemma that is not peculiar to textbook writers but rather is endemic to the entire enterprise of language teaching. On the one hand, we are supposed to teach language, and the most natural instinct historically has been to make this manageable by presenting the different structures (and, more recently, functions) of the language in sequence. The advantage of this is that it ensures that all the important structures are covered; it is also an approach favored by many students used to such syllabi from more traditional language teaching contexts.

On the other hand, however, language is quite meaningless if it is only form and if we have nothing to *say* or *do* with it. Language without content is empty. Several recent philosophies of teaching and learning (for example whole language or process writing) have stressed the need for all language use, including language use in language learning, to be *about* something; in ELT, the content-based movement has championed such an approach. This allows us to focus on the students' responses—for example, to the turkey bowling text mentioned earlier. Yet this approach also has a downside: By always focusing on content, aspects of form may be underemphasized or simply ignored. Students may get to the end of a course, for instance, without ever having looked at certain major grammatical or functional parts of the language. Thus, however much one embraces a philosophy of content, the balance between content and form always has to be considered, because it is in the interests of the students themselves both to have things to say and to have the forms with which to say them. Language teaching materials must also address this balance and take up some position in relation to it.

Naturally, there is a whole lot more that can be said about the values inherent in this textbook or in any other. I have said nothing about lifestyle norms regarding, for example, apartments, cars, and work, that are reflected in the texts and images of the book, or about the image of the student that it discursively constructs, nor about its ideological content; these aspects of ELT materials have been described and analyzed elsewhere (e.g., Canagarajah, 1993). I hope, though, that even in this brief analysis I have given an indication of the rich and conflicting moral messages inscribed in and read from the materials used in ELT classrooms every day across the globe.

Morality in Phonology

Some years ago, I knew a teacher of English in France named Hannah. Hannah was Scottish, and she spoke English with a marked Edinburgh accent; in conversation with me and with other teachers she vigorously defended the value of her variety of English against what today I would label the hegemony of RP or Received Pronunciation, the accent of the upper and upper middle classes of southeastern England which has long been considered the standard pronunciation of British English. Yet Hannah confessed to me at one point that when she taught her French students the pronunciation of English, she changed her accent and taught them RP.

It seems to me that Hannah's decision to teach RP, despite her own beliefs about the equal importance and validity of her own regional form of English, was a moral decision. Furthermore, I mention it here because it highlights a constant issue in our profession: the decision about which form of English we should teach. Although this dilemma extends to all areas of the language—including syntax, lexis, discourse, and pragmatic conventions—I confine my remarks to the area of phonology as being particularly salient and representative.

It is commonly known in our field that the English language includes a bewildering diversity of varieties, especially accents. I was brought up in Lancashire in northwest England. When I was perhaps 8 or 9, during a visit to my grandparents on Tyneside in the northeast, only 100 miles from my own home (Britain is a very small island), I went to play soccer with some of the neighborhood boys. At one point one of them, a little younger than the rest of us, leaned toward his older brother, pointed at me and whispered: "Is he English?"

Since those days, through travel and especially the media, speakers of English all over the world have become somewhat more familiar with different accents and dialects of their own language. Yet this familiarity has done little to change the accents themselves, or attitudes toward them. The problem in the field of ELT is to know which of these varieties to teach.

My contention that this decision is moral in nature—that is, that it is grounded in values—stems from the fact that, as seen from Hannah's own defense of her Scottish accent, language varieties themselves are not value neutral. Quite the opposite, in fact is true: The different varieties of English are highly value laden. Accents are closely linked to the identities of individuals and groups of people; to value one accent over another is, rather directly, to value one group of people over another. The fact that the English of the upper and middle classes of southeast England (the area around London) is seen as the British standard, while that of the working class in the north (where I come from), or of Ireland, or Scotland, or Wales, is not, reflects a broader social notion that the middle-class south is in other ways also the norm or the dominant social group. In other words, this choice of "standard" accent both reflects and reinforces a sociocultural and political hegemony. The same can be said, of course, about regional accents in the United States and other countries, and more broadly about the relationship between British English (or American English) and other varieties of English around the world that have not been accorded the same status—the English of Nigeria, India, or Jamaica, for example.

At the same time, in the teaching and learning of English there are good moral reasons for selecting such a variety and sticking with it. It is probably objectively true that, because of the widespread adoption of RP as a standard (at least in areas where British English is preferred to U.S. English), a student who is taught RP will have fewer problems communicating than one who has been taught to speak with a Scottish accent. It is also probably objectively true that in many educational contexts teachers could get into trouble for teaching what departmental authorities would, rightly or wrongly, see as a marked form of English. Last, while at one level we may rightly wish to make our students aware of the great range of English accents across the world, for pedagogical reasons I would argue rather strongly that it is too much to expect all but the most advanced students to have more than a vague notion of different language varieties, and that for their own good they need to be taught a straightforward and consistent way of pronouncing the language they are learning, with the minimum possible number of variations.

In light of this pedagogical fiat, though, we really do have to choose which variety will serve as the standard to be taught. And here we are faced with a serious moral dilemma. Which form of English are we going to value by making it the standard? How can we determine which variety it will be in the best interests of our students to know and use? This is what I call the *morality of phonology*. There is no easy solution; the matter needs to be given some serious, conscious thought. In many programs and contexts there are certain unspoken assumptions: for example, about the relative "superiority" of American or British English, of American or British "standard" forms over regional accents, or of "center" varieties over "periphery" varieties (Phillipson, 1992). I suggest that in considering the moral meanings underlying pronunciation teaching and the moral messages we send in our teaching it is important to bring these assumptions to light and question them rather than letting the matter be determined by instinctual, unspoken preferences that often arise under particular sociopolitical conditions. Yet at the same time we must acknowledge that by teaching one set of forms over another we may also be reinforcing existing hegemonic relations.

The Moral Substrate of the Process–Product Debate

The final area of conflicting moral values in classroom pedagogy that I look at here is what is sometimes referred to as the *process–product debate* in writing instruction for college-level students. Some years ago, there was an exchange of views on the obligations of second-language writing teachers, in which two principal opposing positions were put forward. One side, which took its cue from research and theory in first-language writing (Elbow, 1973; Emig, 1971; Murray, 1982), argued that writing only had any meaning as expression, and that writing instructors should focus on encouraging writers to express their own views and ideas (Zamel, 1982, 1983). In essence, this movement aimed to give the students *voice* through writing. This approach is known as the process approach because among other things, it pays great attention to the writing process itself: the emergence over time of the writer's ideas, using successive drafts, and seeing the expression of meaning as an emergent product of writing.

The other camp argued that it is the primary duty of the college writing instructor to enable students to succeed in their chosen field by mastering its dominant discourses: that undergraduates in history, for example, need to learn to write like historians (Horowitz, 1986; Swales, 1987). This camp posited that the expectations of professors in the various disciplines are rather rigid, and that it is the job of writing instructors to train students in knowing these expectations and being able to meet them. There is relatively little room for personal freedom of expression, at least as far as form is concerned. Furthermore, in ELT such an approach is particularly needed, because students (e.g., ESL students in British or American universities) will have little prior exposure to the models their teachers expect and are in particular danger of getting it wrong and thus of suffering significant negative consequences. This approach is known as the *product approach*, since it focuses primarily on the formal qualities of the finished piece of writing.

The process–product debate was first discussed some years ago in the ELT literature (Raimes, 1991). Yet the debate itself was never resolved, and it is still very much a central dynamic in the teaching of writing. I argue here that it is a *moral* dynamic, because the underlying opposition it represents is not merely a question of competing classroom methodologies but of values: of what is the good and right thing to do with and for one's students.

The process approach posits the value of voice, or of individual expression, as the most important thing (Taylor, 1992). Of course, teachers who adopt a process approach often emphasize the importance of considering one's audience as one develops a piece of writing and of producing a formally acceptable piece of work at the end of the process. Nevertheless, the goal of the writing process is primarily to lead the writer to express her own ideas, tell her own stories, and give her own views. This approach values the voice of the student as a person and member of the community of the classroom and beyond who has interesting and valuable things to say.

The product approach, however, also has the best interests of the students at heart. Individuals who favor this approach suggest that process teaching is overly idealistic and point out that in the real world, subject-matter teachers are less likely to be interested in the student's voice and more interested in whether she can write in the ways expected in her discipline. This approach can also be said to be grounded in community—the discourse community of the discipline—and in a desire for the student to be able to participate in that community. Advocates of the product approach believe that the interests of the student are best served by enabling her to acquire the language of the academy in general and of particular domains in particular.

Consider an interesting example that shows how one teacher resolved this tension. Xiao-ming Li (1999), a second-language writer of English, told the story of a piece of writing that she produced for a class with Don Murray, a legendary writing instructor at the University of New Hampshire, and then, at Murray's prompting, successfully submitted to *The Boston Globe* newspaper. Li told of when she first gave her work to Professor Murray:

> As I handed in the paper at the end of the class, I was hoping that Murray would correct my writing, but he did nothing. The paper came back bare of any teacherly remarks, only his suggestion that I send it to *The Boston Globe*. That was not what I expected. I expected him to splash the paper with red ink, removing all signs of my foreign accent. I went to Murray's office and insisted on him doing that, even insinuating that he would be seen as a delinquent professor if he did not correct my errors, which I knew were plentiful. But Murray was equally adamant that he should not. What makes the piece interesting, he insisted, is your unique accent, a different perspective, and a different style and voice. And he asked why I should want to sound like a U.S. writer. He pointed out the best writers do not sound like others …. Unconvinced, I continued to pester Murray to go over my paper again and correct the errors. Finally, he changed a few articles and punctuation marks, but would do no more. (p. 49)

In this example, the teacher takes an extreme position in terms of the dynamic mentioned earlier. What he is saying essentially is that Xiao-ming does not have to fit into existing conventions for writing; rather, the reverse is the case: The English language and its literature are enriched and expanded by her contribution. In essence, it is the same argument by which we would say that a writer writing in a dialect or regional variation of English is not writing "incorrect English" but rather is enriching the linguistic and literary culture of English. For myself, the more I think about this argument the more I am convinced that Murray is right. Yet the argument is not always made in ELT and, even setting aside the matter of specific discourse conventions of disciplines, many teachers remain convinced that non-native speakers are unlikely either to make such a contribution or to be accepted in the way Murray accepted Xiao-ming Li as a writer.

Thus, the two approaches outlined here are not merely competing sets of instructional practices; they represent opposing views of what is good and right for the student. The value of voice on the one side is balanced by the value of belonging on the other. My guess is that each individual teacher of writing will constantly weigh these values against each other in every different class. Certainly this is an opposition of which I am very conscious in my own teaching. At times, with particular students it seems to me that I focus on the expressive functions of writing; at others—for example, with the case of Hae-young, described in chapter 1—I decided that the student's ability to understand and use the discourse conventions of the field is more important. In any event, as with the other moral dynamics I have examined in this book, the matter can never be simply resolved once and for all but must be recalculated at each step, with each new learner and each different emerging situation.

THE TEACHER AND THE INSTITUTION: A MORAL DYNAMIC

In this final section I look briefly at a moral dynamic that is rarely if ever broached in education, and certainly not in ELT, yet which I see as playing an often considerable part in the negotiation of moral meanings in the classroom. I am referring to the tension between the teacher's role as an individual versus her role as a representative of the institution for which she works and the broader educational and political systems within which that institution is located.

A recent court case from the realm of general education illustrates the dynamic to which I am referring. An article in my local newspaper ("Court upholds firing,", 2001) reported that an appeals court in Pennsylvania upheld the firing of Bob Brown, a professor at California University of Pennsylvania, for refusing to change a student's grade when told to do so by the president of the university. According to Brown, the student in question "missed 12 of 15 class meetings and did not do most assignments" but was to be given a passing grade for political reasons. In the court case, Brown claimed that "he had a First Amendment right to grade students as he saw fit and to stick by his opinions." The court, however, found otherwise, saying in its decision:

> Because grading is pedagogic, the assignment of the grade is sub-sumed under the university's freedom to determine how a course is to be taught. We therefore conclude that a public university professor does not have a First Amendment right to expression via the school's grade assignment procedures.

I take up the question of grading and its moral meaning in chapter 4. For now, the aspect of this case I wish to highlight is the fact that the court's decision underlines the teacher's identity as representative of a broader insti-tution—and this in an American university setting, where the independence of instructors is usually a point of pride. The professor turns out not to be a free agent; because of his position as a faculty member of a particular institu-tion he is bound by the pedagogical mission of that institution.

A few professionals in TESOL work by and for themselves and are not beholden to any immediate institution—I am thinking of freelance mate-rials writers, those who run their own schools, and so on. Yet the vast major-ity of us work for institutions. These may be public or private schools, language schools, universities, community programs—the list is endless. In every case, however, the moral contours of our work are formed not in a vac-uum but within the context of institutional rules, regulations, customs, and expectations that affect what we do and what we can do in the classroom.

Of course, many teachers have a considerable degree of autonomy in various areas of their work: selecting materials, choosing classroom ac-tivities, and so on. In my own professional career, I have generally been lucky to have had this kind of independence. In many cases, this freedom has not been a deliberate policy (as it is in certain areas in American higher education, for example) but a by-product of the marginalization of the field of ELT; I have also heard many other teachers recounting similar experi-ences. The power and opportunities that come from living on the margins are not to be underestimated or scorned (see chap. 6).

Yet many, many other teachers find that their autonomy is limited in a range of different ways and that their freedom to act on their own part—that is, to engage in the teacher–student relation as themselves—is mitigated by the role they play as representatives of the institutions where they work. In fact, I do not have to go further than my own university for an example. I, as a faculty member, have considerable autonomy to determine the content and manner of my own classes, but many graduate students teaching foreign languages are not so lucky. In one foreign language department in particular, not only are textbooks chosen by the institution, but also the timetable for each day of the semester is firmly set to ensure that all sections of the same class move forward together, a policy that may make administrative sense yet ignores the fact that each learner or group of learners learns differently, and denies the graduate students teaching the classes any kind of autonomy in this regard.

Although this example may seem extreme, I think that many teachers in many contexts will find that it sounds familiar. It is common for teachers to have little or no voice in the selection of course books; the choice of books, in turn, has a huge influence on what happens in classrooms, especially because, as mentioned earlier, course books often form a default curriculum. Furthermore, the institution impinges on classroom interaction in other ways. One powerful arena of influence is that of requirements for grading: While teachers (in most cases) get to determine what grades or marks are assigned, they generally do not have much of a say in overall patterns of evaluation—whether grades are issued at all, for example, or how they are reported. Other such areas include systemic requirements for checking attendance; it was this requirement, for example, that Joe ran up against in his minicourse class described earlier.

What are the moral consequences of our dual roles as individuals and as representatives of our institutions? It seems to me that this duality constitutes another foundational moral dilemma of our work as teachers. We are committed to supporting our students; yet also, in accepting our job, we are committed to upholding the rules of the institutions for which we work. Most teachers can and do break these rules when they see fit, yet we cannot spend the whole of our lives at odds with our institution, for that would make nonsense of our work as teachers.

This situation is made more complicated by the fact that, while human beings are moral agents, institutions are not (Maxwell, 1991), simply because they are not human beings and do not in themselves have agency. The rules and decisions of institutions can and do have moral consequences; yet these are moral only insofar as they affect individuals. Institutions themselves have no moral standing.

This often places us in a peculiar position in relation to our students. For example, Proposition 227, a recently passed law in California, officially removes children from bilingual programs in public schools after they have had a year of bilingual teaching. However, many teachers see that, for a variety of reasons, their children continue to need bilingual education—for example, because they are still not strong enough in English to support education exclusively in that language. As a result, as Varghese (2001a) reported, many teachers in California are still "doing" bilingual education but are having to do it surreptitiously, practicing it in their class without officially declaring they are doing so, and certainly without any funds to support it. I suggest that the decision made by these teachers to continue to teach bilingually is a moral decision: They are convinced that bilingual teaching is in the best interests of their learners and are prepared to break their (perhaps unspoken) contract with their school because the value of supporting the children's needs is more important. Yet this also sets them at odds with the institutions in which they work, at the level of the school, the school district, and the state.

Once again, teachers face complex moral decisions that they themselves must make. Precisely because they are moral agents and their schools are not, at each step they must think about the extent to which the ways the institution impinges on the teacher–student relation are in fact morally tolerable. We all have some wiggle room between the strict enforcement of instructions, rules and regulations that are handed down and what we actually do in our classroom (remember my description in chap. 1 of how I bent to the breaking point the deadline requirements for Hae-Young and her writing assignment), yet as I mentioned before, we cannot blithely disregard every one of these instructions and rules and regulations. Thus, we have to sift through them and decide where we agree with them, where we disagree and wish to take a stand (or simply act in accordance with our convictions, as the California bilingual teachers are doing), and also where we disagree but choose to knuckle down. In other words, some kind of compromise is inevitable, but it is up to each individual teacher to decide in each case what kind of compromise it will be. Whatever decisions are made, even the most dyed-in-the-wool anarchist among teachers cannot fail to acknowledge that she is also a representative of her institution and thus to some extent a carrier, willy-nilly, of its values.

CONCLUSION: MORAL AGENCY IN THE CLASSROOM

My aim in this chapter has been to give some indication of the myriad complex ways in which our actions and decisions in the classroom carry moral meaning. The moral significance of classroom interaction cannot be avoided; it is a foundational part of what we do as teachers. Furthermore, we are not the only moral agents in the classroom: Our students also act in morally meaningful ways, and it is in the interplay between our agency and theirs that the moral essence of the teacher–student relation lies.

I wish to end this section by saying two things. First of all, I believe that reflection on the moral dimensions of classroom interaction offers a vital source of professional growth and understanding for teachers. What emerges for me from this chapter is that the interplay of values in the classroom is always more complex than I might at first imagine; it is crucial to gain some conscious awareness and understanding of the ways in which values and moral judgments are subtly encoded in what is said and done in class.

Second, though I have throughout been emphasizing the complex, ambiguous, and contradictory nature of moral decision making, I do believe firmly that there are better and worse decisions to be made; in other words, that what teachers do and say matters deeply. I have been in too many good and bad classrooms—as a student, as a teacher, or as an observer—to think that all of this uncertainty renders our work meaningless. The problem is not whether our work makes a difference—it does—but that it is never possible to apply blanket rules to situations to determine simplistically what our course of action should be. In every case, we have to re-examine our values and how they play out in the given circumstances; the morality of our decision making lies in the encounter between our own values and the complex details of particular contexts and cases. It is this that makes our work so difficult; yet it is also this that makes it profoundly human and profoundly meaningful.

QUESTIONS FOR REFLECTION AND DISCUSSION

1. What rules for attendance and participation do you have in your classroom? What values underlie these rules? What moral messages might be sent by them? How else might the rules be set up?
2. In discussing the extract from Damon's class, I argued that there is a tension of values between the desire to listen to what students actually have to say and the need for them to "say anything"—to simply keep talking to practice their fluency. What is your perspective on this tension? In your own classes, how do you balance the need to encourage fluency with the need to listen to your learners as people?
3. Have you experienced a situation like the one from Jackie's class, in which a student voices an opinion that is profoundly different from your own values? How did you handle it? What would you have done in Jackie's position? What other ways did she have of responding to the student in question?

4. The following "letter" and "reply," both in fact written by an ESL teacher in the IEP of a midwestern university, appeared in the IEP newsletter aimed at students:

> *Dear Ms. Manners:*
> *I am often homesick and my mother tongue makes me feel warm inside. I love to talk with people who speak my language during the classroom breaks. Sometimes the teacher is still in the room and he tells me to talk in English. The other students seem to agree with him. Nobody seems to understand how hard it is for me here. My teacher made me really angry once by asking me to speak in English at the coffee hour. He does not understand the purpose of the coffee hour. Sincerely, Stranger in a Strange Land.*
>
> Dear Stranger,
> Although Ms. Manners hates to be disagreeable, she must disagree with your criticism of your teacher. Is it possible that you do not understand the purpose of the coffee hour? In the IEP, the coffee hour provides an opportunity for students to practice English in a comfortable atmosphere. That's why the coffee hour is held during class time. If you do not want to speak English, you might try visiting a country where nobody speaks English.
>
> Now, about your homesickness ...   Ms. Manners would like you to remember that most everyone is homesick at some time or another. Ms. Manners misses her mother terribly! Your fellow IEP students are as homesick as you are, and they can help you adjust to life here in B. Try talking about your friends and family at home with your new friends here. You will find that everyone shares a similar problem, and that talking about it in a common language, like English for example, is a great way to feel better. Save your mother tongue for when you call ... well, your mother.

What is your view on what the writer says? How can this advice be reconciled with what was said earlier about voice in the classroom? How might you have responded to a student who raised the question expressed in the letter?

5. Take a look at the coursebook you are currently using. How does it position the learners: To what extent does it encourage their active participation, and to what extent does it treat them

merely as passive receivers of information? What moral messages are encoded in the way the units or chapters of the book are presented?

6. Think about the rules and regulations in force in your classroom that come from your department, school or institution, school district, state, and so on. Do you ever go against these rules? In what circumstances? Do you ever find your own values at odds with the values implicit in the rules you are obliged to follow? What happens in such situations?

3

Values and the Politics of English Language Teaching

Possibly the most significant development in the field of English language teaching (ELT) in the 1990s was the acceptance of the idea that ELT is and always has been a profoundly and unavoidably political undertaking. Since the beginnings of empirical research and theory building in second language learning and teaching in the 1940s and 1950s, there had been an emphasis on language learning as an individual psychological phenomenon. Though proponents of communicative language teaching, the dominant force from the 1970s, acknowledged the importance of communication in the classroom, they still viewed that classroom as an isolated group of individuals whose broader social and political context was irrelevant to the processes of language learning. It was not until the 1980s that researchers, beginning to feel frustrated with the limited understandings of language learning that experimental approaches were yielding, began to turn to ethnographic and other qualitative research methods in an attempt to grasp the fuller realities of language classrooms. The ethnographic approach, in turn, opened our eyes to the myriad ways in which social and political context crucially influences what goes on in classrooms.

At the same time, developments in other disciplines were also leading researchers in language teaching and learning to the "discovery" of the political dimension of language teaching. In philosophy, Michel Foucault's exposés of the socially situated nature of knowledge and of the ways in which knowledge is bound up with the play of power in societal settings, summed up in his concept of "power/knowledge" (Foucault, 1972, 1979, 1980), became a major influence on many social scientific disciplines, including education (e.g., S. J. Ball, 1990; Middleton, 1998; Popkewitz & Brennan, 1998). Elsewhere in education, the work of Paulo Freire (1972) led to the development of critical pedagogy (Giroux, 1988; McLaren, 1989), an approach which I will deal with at greater length later in this chapter. Scholars in the fields of anthropology and sociology began to re-evaluate the apolitical nature of their respective traditions. In linguistics, meanwhile—another doggedly apolitical domain—there was a growing realization of the need for linguists to engage politically, if only to save the object of their inquiries: indigenous and other minority languages, which were disappearing at an alarming rate (Fishman, 1991; Krauss, 1992; Skutnabb-Kangas, 2000).

Although in the 1980s a few individuals did work in critical pedagogy and the politics of language teaching (e.g., Auerbach & Wallerstein, 1987), a much wider awareness of the politics of the field of ELT began with Alastair Pennycook's (1989) article in *TESOL Quarterly* in which he wrote of the "interested"—that is, politically engaged—nature of knowledge and critiqued the distribution of power in the field. This article was ahead of its time; it was not until a few years later that writings on the politics of ELT established themselves as a significant presence in the field. These included Auerbach's (1993) persuasive argument against an English-only policy in the classroom, Benesch's (1993) critique of the "politics of pragmatism" in English as a Second Language (ESL), Canagarajah's (1994) "critical ethnography" of resistance to English in a Sri Lankan classroom, and Willett and Jeannot's (1993) description and analysis of resistance to a critical approach in a teacher education course. Work such as that of Auerbach and Canagarajah also pointed up the links between broader sociopolitical forces and what happens inside the classroom, a theme that has subsequently been taken up more extensively by Coleman (1996), Hall and Eggington (2000), Morgan (1998), Wink (2000), and others. Of central importance in this line of work are books by Pennycook (1994) and Phillipson (1992) that explored in great detail the ways in which English teaching worldwide is saturated with political meaning. More recently, a special issue of *TESOL Quarterly* in the fall of 1999 devoted to "critical approaches to TESOL" placed the politics of ELT center stage in the professional dialogue of the field.

The introduction of the political dimension into our discussions about language teaching has also meant the introduction of a language of values to the field: Where before there was only really the question of what, psycholinguistically speaking, was the most efficient way of acquiring a language, now are matters of ideology, that is, beliefs about values and about what is good and bad, right and wrong, in relation to politics and power relations. At the same time, the values involved, the relations among them, and especially the attitudes toward them of the individuals writing, are rarely made explicit (though see Edge's, 1996a, Paradox 2, referred to in chap. 1).

The purpose of this chapter, then, is to uncover and explore the moral issues that are raised by the realization that language teaching is a political business and by our attempts to address this realization in our work as teachers. First, I outline the specific ways in which teaching is inherently political and examine some of the values at play in this reading of the field. Next, I look in detail at what is probably the single most influential and important response to this reading: critical pedagogy, particularly in its incarnation in ELT. My examination begins with an analysis of the moral issues raised by a particularly interesting case study of critical pedagogy in action: that of Brian Morgan's (1997) article on the politics of pronunciation teaching in an ESL context. After considering the ESL context, I look at the moral questions brought up by the introduction of critical pedagogy in English as a foreign language (EFL) settings—in other words, in countries where English is not a first language. I then offer a critique of critical pedagogy from the perspective of values. Finally, I attempt to sum up the discussion in this chapter by isolating the central moral issue that has been raised and by considering what can be said about the responses of individual teachers to this central dilemma.

HOW ELT IS POLITICAL

Unearthing the Politics of ELT

There are several reasons why the political nature of language teaching went largely unnoticed for so long. First, classrooms do not look at first glance like "political" places. It seems that what is going on in them is simply the learning of another language, a process that at worst is neutral and at best positively benign, bringing all kinds of new benefits to the learners.

Furthermore, most teachers do not think of themselves as political creatures, and many do not believe that classrooms are places where their own political views should be aired. Indeed, many teachers will go out of their way to avoid "sensitive" topics, that is, topics which could lead to serious disagreements among members of the class. This set of topics includes many that are thought of as "political," for example, women's rights, abortion, and capital punishment.

Teachers' own instinctual avoidance of difficult subjects such as these has been supported by trends in communicative language teaching. The vast majority of activities and materials prepared for the communicative classroom are restricted to personal topics such as family, hobbies, and work, or to rather trivial matters. This restriction, in turn, is driven not merely by discomfort but also, as pointed out in chapter 2, by the underlying belief that language teaching is a purely psycholinguistic process and that so long as "communication" is occurring and language is being spoken and heard, it does not really matter what that communication is about (so long as a variety of grammatical structures, lexis, and pragmatic functions are being used). It is also reinforced by the reluctance of publishers of ELT textbooks and course books to include any materials that might be deemed offensive by certain populations of learners.

A final reason why teaching was long seen as apolitical is that the people who benefited most from the political role of language teaching were not those directly involved in it. While teachers, administrators, teacher trainers, and researchers may make a living from language teaching, most of them are not wealthy. On the other hand, individuals whose interests are served by particular practices in language education—politicians, businesspeople, and religious leaders—do not take part in the day-to-day work of teaching languages.

Part of the invisibility of the politics of language teaching arises from an overly narrow understanding of the term *political*. For most people, this term applies only to the making of laws by national and local officials, the election of those officials, the credos and actions of political parties, relations among national governments, and so on. Yet in fact the term *political* has a much broader field of reference. It refers to anything that has to do with power and the control of resources of every conceivable kind. In this understanding, a great many things about language teaching are political. In fact, there is an interesting parallel with morality: Just as in chapter 1 I discussed the distinction between the teaching of morality and the morality of teaching, so here we can think in terms of the teaching of politics versus the politics of teaching.

Yet another problem is the fact that teachers are rarely encouraged to reflect on the broader sociopolitical context in which they work. As we see in a moment, an important aspect of the political nature of ELT inheres in its role in large-scale societal processes, such as colonization and globalization, yet teachers are not often urged to conceptualize their work at the level of its relation to national political, economic, and cultural processes.

ELT and Politics

How, then, is ELT political, exactly? There are many ways in which teaching can be thought of as political in nature. In this section I briefly outline five clearly political aspects of ELT: the part played by language education in the processes of colonization and decolonization, the effect of the spread of English on indigenous languages, the political dimension of teaching immigrant and refugee learners in ESL contexts, the dominance of English in the media and in computer-based technologies, and the role of English in globalization.

The spread of English has been intimately associated with the processes of colonization and decolonization and the vast machineries of economic, political, and cultural hegemony that have attended it. Phillipson (1992) and Pennycook (1994) both have offered detailed accounts of the ways in which the teaching of English in African contexts and in southeast Asia, respectively, were a vital part of the mechanism of colonialism. Other writers have explored similar relations in various colonial and postcolonial contexts. Furthermore, English has also been a constant feature in the subsequent processes of decolonization in countries from South Africa (Eastman, 1990) to Sri Lanka (Canagarajah, 1993): The English-speaking powers that be have been anxious to maintain the ascendancy of the English language as colonial paternalism is replaced by more subtly hegemonic relations. Thus, while present-day teachers are not living in the "bad old days" of untrammeled colonialism, it is still very much the case that the teaching of English is one important mechanism whereby the old subservient relations are *de facto* maintained and perpetuated.

The predatory action of English is nowhere more evident than in the effect of the spread of English on indigenous languages. As a direct result of the imposition of English, literally dozens of languages are dying in the United States alone as I write this paragraph. The shift from the hard power of boarding schools and banned languages to the soft power of neglect and what Michael Krauss called the "cultural nerve gas" (1992, p. 8) of television and other media has done little to halt, let alone reverse, this process. The figures are appalling: Krauss estimated that in the next 200 years up to 90% of the world's languages could be irretrievably lost (see also Skutnabb-Kangas, 2000). From everything I have personally seen and read, I cannot regard this estimate as an exaggeration. Although at an intellectual level the loss of whole languages and cultures is a terrible thing, from a moral perspective one of the most appalling aspects of this situation is the devastating effect of the process of language shift on actual individuals and their familial and social relations.

Another domain in which politics blatantly enters the language classroom is that of teaching English to adult and child immigrants in the United States, Canada, the United Kingdom, Australia, New Zealand, and elsewhere. Here there is little danger that the Spanish or Vietnamese or Polish languages will disappear wholesale. Yet, as with the case of indigenous languages, a moral standpoint reminds us that it is actual people who matter, not languages as abstract things; and individual people suffer greatly at the jerking shift from their first language to English, the language of the new country (Igoa, 1995). When children are educated exclusively in their second language or in a bilingual system of the subtractive or replacement kind in which the first language is gradually faded out, they literally lose contact with older generations of their family and community. The parents and grandparents, on the other hand, also find themselves not merely culturally but also linguistically at odds with their children.

The rapidly growing importance of computer-based technologies, and especially of the Internet and the World Wide Web, has constituted another area in which the spread of English has considerable political significance. An inordinate percentage of websites and electronic communications are in English. There are people, of course, who argue that the Web represents a democratization of communication and that it is capable of actually reversing the spread of English (Wallraff, 2000). This may be a theoretical possibility, but the present reality is that the Web is contributing to the same forces of social, economic, and cultural inequality as those of colonialism and postcolonialism mentioned earlier. The very use of, and access to, computers serves to separate rich and poor ever more; those who have access to them are in the vast majority of cases speakers of English or another dominant world language (Spanish, German, French, Chinese, Russian, Japanese, Arabic). These processes affect ELT in several ways, at least two of which are worth mentioning here: the increasingly widespread use of computers for tests such as the Test of English as a Foreign Language (TOEFL) and the consuming obsession many teachers, teacher trainers, and materials writers have developed with using computers to teach English.

The use of English on the Internet is one example of a much broader process that is usually referred to as *globalization* (Giddens, 2000; Mittelman, 2000); this process is also profoundly political in nature, and ELT is also profoundly implicated in it (Phillipson, 1992; Spring, 1998). This is true if only because globalization is forever being appealed to as a motivation for learners in EFL contexts to learn English. At the same time, for good or for bad, globalization is possibly the most significant political force of the present age. Within all of this, the business of ELT goes on in increasingly globalized ways. First, there is more physical mobility: More and more native speakers are traveling to teach abroad, while increasing numbers of non-native speaker teachers are able both to travel to English-speaking countries and to get training there. Second, there is what might be called *economic mobility*: With the gradual erasure of national boundaries in economic terms, a process aggressively supported by the financial powers that be (e.g., GATT, the General Agreement on Tariffs and Trades), Western companies are increasingly able to exploit foreign markets (the reverse, of course, much less frequently being the case); this allows American and British textbook companies to market their wares much more extensively and intensively than ever before, in a rapidly growing number of countries (witness, for example, the invasion of former Eastern bloc countries by companies such as Longman, Cambridge University Press, Oxford University Press, or Heinemann in the years immediately following 1989). Third, there is virtual mobility: the increasing ease of communication by various hi-tech means. The overall result of this is that computer users have to use English to access and connect with the rest of the world (often meaning the United States), while television viewers in pretty much any country in the world can watch CNN and MTV in English (whereas in the United States, with a few regionalized exceptions, it is, virtually, impossible to watch television in other languages).

In all these areas, then, English, the spread of English, and the teaching of English can be seen to have profound political significance. In each case I have either hinted at, or indicated outright, some of the moral underpinnings of this political significance. In the rest of this section I suggest the complexity and depth of the politics of language teaching by exploring one of the areas in detail. I look at two stories regarding the teaching of indigenous languages: one experience of my own and another recounted to me by a former student.

Politics and Values in the Practice of Language Education: Two Examples

I wrote earlier that teachers are, generally speaking, not encouraged to think about the political meaning of their work in language teaching. However, it has consistently been my experience that when teachers *are* asked to reflect on this issue they find themselves faced with conflicts of values, that is, with moral quandaries.

If one hangs around in universities and at conferences of applied linguists, the notion of supporting the revitalization of indigenous languages usually seems, as my teenage daughter would put it, a no-brainer. Of course we applied linguists support programming in indigenous languages, just as we support bilingual education and other multicultural practices. We have all seen "Dances With Wolves"; we all agree that Indians, and other indigenous groups around the world, have suffered terribly at the hands of European colonists; of course the teaching of indigenous languages should be supported.

However, when one is, so to speak, on the ground, it is often far from clear what the good and right course of action is, even when one's views are firm and strong. In fact, the matter of teaching indigenous languages, like any other political area of language teaching, is fraught with moral dilemmas and conflicts of values.

One of my former students, Kay, is currently working for a church organization setting up village schools in rural areas of the Central African Republic. While Kay was in Bloomington, we spoke of the vital importance of maintaining indigenous languages not just in the United States but all around the world, and of the predacious effects of the unchecked teaching of colonial or postcolonial languages. Yet now that Kay is in the Central African Republic, she finds that there is hardly any support locally for such values and that, given the staggering lack of resources, it is a colossal struggle even to institute French-language schooling. As she wrote to me in a recent e-mail:

> What can I even say about the language issue? There is an overwhelming push ("overwhelming" is even an understatement) for French in the schools—practically speaking, I am centuries away from getting anyone to hear anything about mother tongue education or even literacy. All I am hoping for now is for a way to use the MT [mother tongue](orally) to help and not hinder French acquisition as well as other content. I think classes here are and always have been "bilingual" in reality—no teacher can really make do with TOTAL French immersion here. How do I train these teachers to promote French language skills, French reading skills, and all other skills supposedly in the French medium, so that all these non-francophone little kids actually learn something in the end?

Kay faces an ongoing moral dilemma: How much of her limited time, energy, and resources should she devote to a cause that she knows is right but unlikely to produce results in that particular context—that of promoting indigenous language education? To what extent should she compromise and concentrate on establishing education in a European language, knowing on the one hand that this will probably be the villagers' only hope of access to any kind of education for their children, yet on the other hand that she is participating in a global process which sooner or later may well have highly deleterious consequences for the local culture, and that further-more, though everyone is free to hope, for these villagers even access to French may not necessarily mean access to a better life (Rogers, 1982)? This is what I mean by the moral complexity of language teaching, for it is with dilemmas such as this that language teachers have to wrestle every day.

My second example comes from some work I myself did in the area of indigenous language revitalization; I described this work in more detail elsewhere (B. Johnston, in press). From 1998 to 2000, I worked with a Da-kota community on an Indian reservation in Minnesota as they developed a preschool immersion program for the Dakota language. I was profoundly committed to this program, because it embodies values that I held, and still hold, very dear both professionally and personally. Like many in our field, I strongly support efforts to stabilize, maintain, and revitalize indigenous lan-guages. I further believe that as an applied linguist I have a professional duty to engage in this work whenever I am given the opportunity and that I have some knowledge, skills, and understanding that may be helpful.

The program opened in October 1999. Though on a small scale, it appeared to be about to take off. The program was run in a highly profes-sional manner by a Dakota educator named Angela Wilson, who had gone to great efforts to ensure both that the school embodied Dakota cultural values and that, pedagogically speaking, it was structured to maximally encourage language acquisition. The teachers in the program were Dakota elders, supported by younger non-Dakota yet Dakota-speaking aides. Through the first 6 months of the program, the children, aged 1–5, gradu-ally grew in their receptive and spoken ability in the language.

However, the program was also riven by political conflicts. Sev-eral of the teaching elders resented the fact that the program was being run by a younger person, and a woman to boot; furthermore, they found it diffi-cult to enact some of the pedagogical strategies Angela and I suggested, and claimed that certain aspects of the program—for example, the process (which Angela encouraged) of creating new words to avoid the use of Eng-lish for modern technological inventions and other things—were un-Da-kota. There was also a strong undercurrent of resentment against the White teacher's aides. To cut a long story short, the atmosphere became intolera-ble and, lacking the crucial support of the Tribal Council, Wilson resigned as director at the end of March 2000, thus effectively bringing about the end of the program.

The most important and tragic aspect of this affair, of course, is the fact that the children in the program no longer have access to education in their own ancestral language. For my purposes here, though, I wish to focus for a moment on the moral underpinnings of the story, specifically as these relate to my role in it.

I already explained that my involvement in this program—as a consultant and teacher trainer—was based in values that I hold dear: the nobility and vital importance of the struggle to prevent languages from disappearing from the face of the earth. Yet in the real context of the Dakota reservation where I was working, I found a much more complex moral landscape emerging. First, although I thought I was committed to "the Dakota," I found many of the people with whom I worked and interacted resented, to a greater or lesser extent, my role as a White "expert" brought in from outside. In one sense, to be true to my own belief in the rights of indigenous peoples to self-determination, I should simply have left, respecting their wishes and allowing them to rely on their own expertise. Another way of putting this is to say that, while I believe I know something about how to organize the learning of languages, I also have a belief in the value of alternative ways of knowing, and I would not claim that the Western or White forms of knowledge in which I trade at the university are superior to other forms of knowledge. On the other hand, from everything I have both read and experienced about language growth and language learning, I do believe that I was right—for example, to argue for interactive ways of working with the children and for the value of helping the language to grow by consciously creating new vocabulary. I believed, and still believe, that the approaches Angela and I were suggesting offered the best chance for the Dakota language to survive.

In the end, though, I remained in the project because Angela and other Dakota continued to ask me to be involved. This presented another quandary: Which Indians were right? I knew who I sided with, but there was no clear-cut sense in which I was supporting "the Dakota." The community was divided; the romantic image of the tribe as a single group united behind the goal of reviving the language was a fiction.

What was I to do, then? Ply my wares and push for an interactive approach when I knew this ran against the expectations of many of the participants? Or accept in a spirit of respect what was claimed to be the "Dakota way," which I believed would not lead to effective language learning? These dilemmas were cut short by the termination of the program, but I continue to mull over them as I reflect on White involvement in community programs of this sort. The brutal truth here, at least as I see it, is that this program represented by far the best opportunity the community had to keep the Dakota language alive. The values of maintaining the language and of respecting the culture and its most important bearers, the elders, come into terrible conflict here: To this day I do not know how that conflict can be resolved, even by the Dakota themselves, let alone by White experts from outside.

My overall message is that the two examples mentioned here are not isolated or unusual cases, but on the contrary that the field of indigenous language programming, like any area of teaching, is played out amid difficult and deep-reaching moral conflicts and clashes of values. A common element to these two stories is the clash between what insiders believe to be the right and good thing to do and what the outsider teacher considers to be good and right. This conflict is echoed in various forms throughout the different contexts of language teaching.

ONE RESPONSE: CRITICAL PEDAGOGY

An Introduction to Critical Pedagogy

Critical pedagogy is an approach to teaching that not only acknowledges the political dimension of education but places that dimension center stage in calling for a politically committed pedagogy. Critical pedagogists believe in "the centrality of politics and power in our understanding of how schools work" (McLaren, 1989, p. 159). Pennycook (1994) summed up critical pedagogy as "education grounded in a desire for social change" (p. 297).

Critical pedagogy calls for the "empowerment" of learners. This is achieved through a variety of means. One is a commitment to student voice. Another is an ongoing process of helping learners to understand that the "knowledge" they are taught in school is not necessarily objective and neutral but "interested" and socially constructed, and to support students in becoming producers, not merely consumers, of knowledge. Another means is the use of class activities that encourage the process of "conscientization" (Freire, 1972, p. 15), that is, making students aware both of the political dimension of their situation and of their capacity for acting on that situation politically and working toward a vision of a better world. It is thus a pedagogy not merely of discussing the political but of taking action. Furthermore, as is implicit in this brief description, it is a pedagogy that calls on teachers to be open about their political views and engaged in political activity. Once again, we need to remember that political activity means not working for a political party but rather becoming aware of the ways power operates in the world and taking action to redress inequities.

Critical pedagogy has its roots in the teachings of Paulo Freire (1972), who used this approach to teach literacy to Brazilian peasants and simultaneously to lead those peasants to reflect on their situation of oppression and subsequently to work to improve it. Freire's ideas were embraced in Western K–12 teaching by Henry Giroux (1988), Peter McLaren (1989), Ira Shor (1996), and many others. Over the last 10 or 15 years, they have become part of the discourse of ELT: Pennycook (1994, 2001) and others have developed theoretical arguments, while teachers and teacher educators such as Auerbach (1993), Morgan (1998), Benesch (1993), and Crookes and Lehner (1998) have attempted to flesh out the theory and develop appropriate classroom practices. Thus far critical pedagogy has been most widely practiced in North American adult ESL classrooms; however, there have been repeated calls for critical practices in EFL contexts and elsewhere (e.g., Pennycook, 1994, pp. 295–327).

To conclude this very brief overview, I wish to point out that critical pedagogy is of interest to me for two reasons. First, as already mentioned, it is the only approach in ELT that has made any sustained attempt to address the undeniable political significance of the field. Second, whatever else one might say about it, it is an approach that is profoundly and overtly anchored in values. I argue that the underlying implication, or perhaps assumption, of the theoretical literature is that teachers should be led to embrace critical pedagogy because of their own values, that is, for moral reasons. I am struck by the fact that both Paulo Freire and Nel Noddings, two otherwise very different thinkers, assign central importance to *dialogue*—that is, the moral relation between teacher and student—in educational relations (Freire, 1972; Noddings, 1984). Also, of the nine principal features of critical pedagogy that Pennycook (1994) cited from Giroux (1991), the second is that

> Ethics needs to be understood as central to education, suggesting that the issues we face as teachers and students are not just questions of knowledge and truth but also of good and bad, of the need to struggle against inequality and injustice. (Pennycook, 1994, p. 298)

As I explain later, I believe there is what might be termed *logical slippage* in this argument. I do not practice critical pedagogy myself, but I have a high regard for this approach, and in the following discussion I attempt to examine some of the moral dynamics underlying the practice and theory of critical pedagogy.

A Case Study of Critical Pedagogy in an ESL Setting

As I mentioned earlier, much of the best work in critical pedagogy for ELT has been done in ESL settings, especially in adult education. From Auerbach and Wallerstein's (1987) practical teaching materials to empirical research and program descriptions by Morgan (1998), Rivera (1999), Frye (1999), and many others, there has been a sustained effort to build a theoretically sound and practically viable critical approach to the teaching of English to adults in ESL contexts. For this reason, as I explained earlier, in order to best examine the political dimension of language teaching, and to explore its moral substrate, I focus here on an example of critical pedagogy in action in such a context.

The example I have chosen is the work described by Brian Morgan (1997) in his article entitled "Identity and Intonation: Linking Dynamic Processes in an ESL Classroom." I feel that this will be an effective way of exploring the moral dilemmas and conflicts of values that dwell in critical pedagogy and, more broadly, in any attempt to deal with political matters in the ESL classroom. In presenting Morgan's work I set aside his (very interesting and well-presented) discussion of sociolinguistic and phonological theory and focus on what he actually did with his class.

Morgan (1997) described a 2-day pronunciation activity he conducted with a group of adult learners in a community ESL program in Toronto, Ontario, Canada. The learners were all Chinese speakers and were predominantly older female immigrants from Hong Kong. The first day of class began with the following vignette from the students' textbook:

> Yuen-Li is the wife of Chian-Li. They have been in the United States for two years. Chian-Li is very traditionally minded, believing that a wife should stay at home, make herself beautiful for him, and look after their two teenaged children, Steve and Sue. The family always speaks Cantonese at home, and Yuen-Li doesn't know any English. Chian-Li has attended English classes because sometimes he needs English in his job. He is an importer. Yuen-Li feels very isolated. (Bowers & Godfrey, 1985, p. 25, cited in Morgan, 1997, p. 440)

The rest of this first class was devoted to a group activity that involved ranking a number of different solutions to Yuen-Li's "problem", including the following:

Solution No. 1: Try to explain to her husband that she, too, would like to take English classes.

Solution No. 2: Ask her children to try to convince Chian-Li that she should go to English classes.

Solution No. 3: Explain to Chian-Li that her lack of English will have a bad effect on the family.

Solution No. 4: Go to English classes during the day, and hope that Chian-Li will be pleased when he discovers that she has learned the language. (Morgan, 1997, p. 441)

Morgan (1997) reported that this discussion was very lively and included a number of interesting dynamics. For example, two of the four men in the class said they would be angry if their wives chose Solution 4, whereas half the women in the class felt that this was the best solution. During the discussion the participants, both men and women, expressed various views on the social position and status of women—one of the men, for example, believed that in Canada women have "more power" than men.

For the following day, Morgan (1997) decided to build a pronunciation lesson around Solution 4 "because it had generated the most discussion and opposing viewpoints the day before" (p. 442). He brought to class the following dialogue he had prepared:

Yuen: Sue, would you mind helping me cook dinner?

Chian: Yuen, you're speaking English. How did you learn those words?

Yuen: Oh, I've been studying at a community center for several months. I really enjoy it, and the teacher is very good.

Chian: You should have told me first. You know that the customs here are different and you might cause some trouble for us.

Yuen: I'm sorry, Chian. But you're so busy, and I didn't want to trouble you. Besides, the lessons are free, and many other Chinese housewives are in the class.

Chian: Well then, I think everything will be fine as long as you don't forget your duties for the family. (p. 442–443)

Morgan used this dialogue to practice different options for intonation, explaining the import of each option in terms of the relationship between Yuen and Chian—for example, the different ways the word *oh* could be pronounced to indicate uncertainty, fear, or covert resistance (p. 443). Students practiced the dialogue in pairs; each pair then produced a new dialogue on the same theme and presented it to the rest of the class.

What most interests me as far as this chapter is concerned is something Morgan (1997) wrote in his Conclusions section:

> It would be inappropriate to tell students how to conduct their family
> lives in Canada. At the same time, I believe, it would be irresponsible
> not to teach them how to "say dangerous things" wherever and when-

ever they need to do so. As an ESL teacher, I am keenly interested in the full yet unrealized potentials of language. Sometimes language is a thing of beauty, sometimes a model of clarity and precision, and sometimes a weapon. All local options of language should be made available to newcomers in our society—if not for personal use, then at least for scrutiny and recognition when their interests as newcomers are at stake. (p. 446)

It is in this passage that Morgan (1997) touched on the moral meaning of his lessons. I would like to explore this dimension of his classes more closely.

My students and I read Morgan's (1997) article in my methods classes. Usually, a fair number of the students find it rather shocking, and they protest. They argue that Morgan is wrong to "mess with other people's cultures." From my point of view, however, the matter is much more complex. To begin with, as I suggested in chapter 1, it seems obvious to me that *all* ELT is "messing with other people's cultures," whether we like it or not. Especially in the case of ESL for immigrant and refugee students, a large part of what we do involves explaining, justifying, and engaging with the cultural practices of the students' new homeland.

Given this inevitability, the teacher always takes *some* kind of action, regardless of whether it is conscious or intentional. Furthermore, the action is usually based, consciously or otherwise, on values held by the teacher. A teacher who chooses not to raise matters of sociopolitical standing and power relations in the family is not being apolitical but is merely placing the value of noninterference above other values (Benesch, 1993). The interesting thing about Morgan's (1997) work is that he makes this choice very explicit. His decision to raise these issues, and to do so in such detail, is a *moral* choice: He believes that it is the right thing for him as a teacher to do in this particular situation.

Yet, like any choice, Morgan's (1997) decision has complex and contradictory moral outcomes that he can only partly know. What will be the consequences of his decision for the women (and the men) in his class? To what extent can the teacher be held responsible for these consequences? Morgan has chosen to act on the world in a way that he believes to be right, yet his actions may—indeed, almost certainly will—have consequences both good and bad that he was utterly unable to anticipate.

Furthermore, Morgan's (1997) claim that he is not telling his students how to conduct their family lives is somewhat disingenuous, in two respects. First, Morgan does in fact make his own views rather clear. For example, when the male student mentioned earlier claims that women have "more power," Morgan states that he attempted "to draw out opinions and experiences that would challenge his assumption and help indicate the constraints—the absence of power—that compel some women to stay in low-paying jobs" (pp. 441– 442). Thus, like Jackie in chapter 2, Morgan made his own views known without having to explicitly state them, and he did so in the belief that it was the right and good thing to do.

Second, while it is true that Morgan (1997) did not tell his students how to interact with their spouses, the very fact of bringing this matter up in class is a cultural act in itself. By doing so, he was supporting an open discussion of things that otherwise might remain unsaid; and such forms of discussion themselves constitute a value.

It is important, on the other hand, to dispel two notions. First, the idea of the teacher influencing these—or any—students is a gross oversimplification. Especially when teaching adults, although on the one hand all that we do constitutes action on the world, students are agents in their own right and are not mechanistically manipulated by the teacher. Second, it is of limited use here to appeal to "Chinese cultural norms." Such norms, as Morgan (1997) showed in the case of Yuen-Li, are in many cases contested sites for those subject to them. Far from being inexorable forces, these norms can be resisted in various ways. This is all the more true in ESL contexts, where, quite independent of teachers and education programs, the entire host culture represents a massive sustained challenge to many of the values brought in by immigrants.

This, in turn, brings us back to one of the fundamental conflicts of values underlying ESL teaching (Edge, 1996a). On the one hand, like Morgan, we teachers of ESL and EFL profess a respect for alternative cultural values and undertake not to impose our own values on others. On the other hand, also like Morgan, we hold certain of our own cultural values so dear that we want them to guide our work: For example, Morgan (1997) believes in the value of dialogue and that he has a duty to teach his students how to "say dangerous things" and to prepare them linguistically to protect their own interests in their new country. Such linguistic behavior most certainly contravenes values of the other culture, as Morgan's own work and my analysis clearly indicate.

Thus Morgan—like every other ESL teacher—has to make complex decisions that require irreconcilable conflicts of values to be somehow overcome. Ultimately, decisions are always made; sometimes they are overtly and consciously based in values, as in the case of Morgan's work, but they always have moral meaning, and they always involve moral dilemmas.

Critical Pedagogy and Politics in EFL Contexts

The politics of ELT is one thing in ESL settings. It is quite another in EFL contexts, that is, in contexts where English is not the ambient first language but is a foreign language. Again using the lens of critical pedagogy, in this section I examine some of the moral consequences of addressing the political dimension in EFL education.

I begin from my own context. For me, the question of critical pedagogy in EFL raises moral issues in my own work as a teacher educator. In my methods classes my students and I read about critical pedagogy, and I explain my reasons for saying that all education is political in nature. In many (though by no means all), cases students find the arguments persuasive. However, I immediately find myself faced with a series of moral dilemmas. First, to what extent should I recommend to international students that they consider embracing critical pedagogy in their teaching in their own countries? On the one hand, I myself remain unconvinced that a critical approach is defensible (B. Johnston, 1999b). On the other hand, I acknowledge the importance of political issues in education and thus the impact that this inevitably has on one's pedagogy; to date, at least, critical pedagogy is the best option we have.

Furthermore, in considering what to say to the international students I wrestle with another incarnation of the same moral dynamic that crops up over and again in this book. As one who professes respect for other cultures and values, I am reluctant to make recommendations regarding the ways members of other cultures should behave within their own cultural settings. On the other hand, not only is everything I do indirect action on their worlds, but also it is my *job* to influence my students and to change the way they teach—if I did not do so, my work as a teacher educator would not be successful. Many of these students come to the United States precisely because they are dissatisfied with aspects of their own teaching, and they turn to me for guidance. If I believe that teaching in any context must be somehow politicized, I would be selling myself and them short if I did not bring this up in class. Last, while I have respect for other cultures and their values, like Brian Morgan in the previous section, I also have a set of beliefs that I personally hold to be universal, including the equality of men and women and of people of different races, the right of peoples to self-determination, and the right of individuals to self-expression. There is often a fine line between respecting other cultures and transgressing the integrity of one's own views, yet there is also a fine line between being open about one's views and treating those views as if they are, or should be, universal.

These, however, are my own personal moral dilemmas as a teacher educator. As I mentioned earlier, many critical pedagogists have called for critical pedagogical approaches to be extended to EFL situations. I was recently asked to contribute a talk about critical pedagogy in EFL settings to a colloquium on critical approaches to ELT. I decided that while my own moral misgivings were all very absorbing, it would be much more interesting to hear the perspectives of my students. In the fall 2000 semester, after the classes in which my students and I had discussed critical pedagogy, I asked them to write a journal entry about whether and how critical pedagogy could and should be applied in the national setting with which they were most familiar. I saw this as a kind of thought experiment in which they imagined what would happen if they used a critical pedagogical approach in their home country.

The responses were indeed very interesting and represented a wide range of arguments and positions. I now look briefly at three responses, all by female teachers, from Japan, Thailand, and Brazil.

Given the traditional argument that expatriate teachers should be particularly cautious about introducing new ideas and approaches in contexts with which they are not familiar, I found it particularly striking that Harumi, the Japanese teacher, argued quite the opposite: that in Japan it would be more culturally acceptable for a foreigner than for a native Japanese teacher to engage in critical pedagogy. Harumi observed that because in Japan "foreigners are treated as outsiders" and "can never be society members," this paradoxically makes it easier for them to take innovative approaches, although "[o]f course, an individual effort by foreign teachers is too small to change the mainstream." However, Harumi presented a series of reasons why it would be difficult for a Japanese teacher to introduce critical pedagogy. Foremost among these was that "it would have conflict with teacher–student relations." There were several aspects to this. Harumi explained that "in Japanese culture, there is a clear boundary between teachers and students, and the teachers are supposed to have dignity enough to keep the boundary existing." She anticipated that critical pedagogy would run counter to this expectation. In addition, a teacher introducing critical pedagogy is likely to run into conflicts with other teachers, who expect their colleagues not to stand out by using a different methodology and who might resent it if the students showed a preference for the new method (and thus for that teacher). Last, she felt that "since many Japanese children are told to respect their teachers, they would be confused by too much freedom in [the] Critical Pedagogy classroom."

In thinking about Harumi's comments, I was struck by the fact that moral concerns seemed to underlie her response. First, her objections are couched primarily in terms of teacher–student relations, and these relations, I have repeatedly argued, are moral in nature (see chapter 1). Second, Harumi's remarks once again place us, as ELT professionals, in a cross-cultural moral quandary. Do we want to say that freedom is an absolute good? If so, what do we have to say about respect? Do we want to claim that Western ways of doing things are better than the Japanese ways? It seems to me that for those who believe critical pedagogy is right for EFL settings, this claim must eventually be made; yet it immediately places the critical pedagogist at odds with the most deeply ingrained values of the profession.

The moral foundation of Harumi's response to critical pedagogy can also be seen in the two other responses I look at here. In her reply to my request, Panida, from Thailand, told me a story from her experiences as an EFL teacher at a new university in Thailand. She wrote about a class of students who took part in a special program which, though it did not constitute critical pedagogy, contained certain key elements of it: Going clearly against the grain of traditional teaching in Thailand, this program emphasized critical thinking, the need to challenge written authority, and the importance of being able to express one's own views. The program had considerable success in its goal of improving the students' language abilities and self-confidence. However, it also led to complaints by other teachers (who did not teach English), who found the students overly critical of anything and everything in their courses and not sufficiently respectful, that after "their close contact with their American teacher ... they treated teachers as friends on all occasions." Panida observed that the root of the problem lay in what she saw as a failure on the part of the program: "Not only we would like our students to be good at English, but also we hoped for them to be a good and responsible person in our Thai cultural contexts." In reflecting on the students' tendency to pick fault, Panida asked herself: "Have we trained them to be too expressive?" And she concluded that "we did a sufficiently good job in language training, but failed the morality part." Once again, we see in general how matters of language teaching are linked so deeply and in such a complex fashion with questions of values and specifically how these questions of values arise from the politics and power relations of cultural settings.

The third teacher, Ana, from Brazil, was more hopeful about the applicability of critical pedagogy. Speaking of the increasing presence of English and English-language cultural phenomena (such as McDonald's restaurants) in Brazil, she concluded:

> The massive presence of English in everyday life and the fact that it is practically mandatory for economic and social ascendancy trig-

gers a negative feeling of oppression that my students, particularly
the adolescent ones, have many times talked about informally outside of class. In such a situation, it seems more than timely to apply
critical pedagogy in English teaching, as it gives the learners a
voice with which they can talk back and position themselves as active participants in society.

Here, while Ana's conclusions about the appropriateness of a critical approach are quite different from those of Harumi and Panida, her reasoning is also rooted in moral relations: In this case, her belief in the need
to engage in political issues arises from a belief in the moral rightness of
giving the students voice and thus supporting their empowerment. The
moral underpinnings of her position are confirmed later when she views
the situation from her own perspective as teacher. She wrote: "As teachers
we have to analyze our ethics, and given the social, economic and political
situation of my EFL experience, I cannot assume a neutral position and ignore the context in which English is situated in Brazil." Here again it is a
moral imperative that leads the teacher to take a particular stand on the role
of politics in the English classroom, even though, as can be seen, Ana's response in the Brazilian context is entirely different from that of Harumi in
the Japanese context or Panida in the Thai setting.

The politics of English teaching in EFL settings is a complex and
problematic business in which cultural and individual values loom large,
and although acknowledging the political dimension of language education in such settings is relatively easy, it seems to me that the decision
about whether, and to what extent, each individual teacher feels it right to
embrace critical pedagogy is above all a moral question—that is, a matter
of values—that can and must be left only to that teacher.

As a kind of coda, I would like to add that as I worked on this section I found myself reflecting on my own experience in Poland, where during the 1980s I worked for the best part of 6 years under the Communist
regime. Our lives both in and out of teaching were highly politicized in those
days; we felt the sting of power relations in everything from the ration cards
we had to use to buy meat, sugar, and other basic goods, to the outrageous
prevarications of the government during the Chernobyl crisis of 1986, when
radioactive rainclouds passed over the city where I was living with my wife
and children. Furthermore, outside of class my students (who were university faculty) and I talked politics a great deal, and I knew many people involved with the outlawed Solidarity organization, including a large number
who had served jail time under martial law just a couple of years earlier. Yet
in class it would have been both foolish and pointless to address political is-

sues with the fervor and commitment that we had in our private conversa-tions. At the time I had not heard of critical pedagogy; but I think that if I had, I would have seen it as an idealistic and dangerously oversimplified ap-proach to a very complex problem. People in Poland knew full well what the political score was: It would be both ridiculous and insulting to suggest that they were unaware of their own oppression. Furthermore, all of us sincerely believed in the importance of social change. Under those conditions, how-ever, only a certain amount of action was possible. The reason I did not "do politics" in class was that it would be dangerous for myself and, above all, my immediate and extended family. Today, certain of my students come from regimes not entirely dissimilar to that of Communist Poland or repres-sive in ways that are different yet equally difficult to deal with. I find it very hard to urge these teachers to take an overtly political line in their teaching.

Critical Pedagogy Reassessed

As I have explained elsewhere (B. Johnston, 1999b), I am not entirely con-vinced by critical pedagogy. I have several objections, all of which have a moral coloring. First, I find a lot of writing about critical pedagogy to be too abstract, theoretical, and couched in exclusionary language; in this I believe that many theorists have failed in their moral obligation to make their ideas fully accessible to others, especially practicing teachers. Sec-ond, I resent the posturing that accompanies a lot of the theoretical work in mainstream education (and is mercifully absent in most critical pedagogi-cal writings in ELT); this writing claims the moral high ground in debates over the political nature of schooling, and I believe that such a claim does not support the best interests of teachers and learners (Janangelo, 1993).

My primary point of disagreement with critical pedagogy, how-ever, is not so much an intellectual objection as a difference of axiomatic starting points. While Giroux, McLaren, Pennycook and others see teach-ing as above all involving issues of politics and power, my view is that the most basic quality of teaching is its moral dimension. The ways in which political interests and power relations exist in all educational contexts is of very great importance; I have tried to underline this fact by placing the present chapter near the beginning of my book. However, my view of teaching rests ultimately on a different assumption. At heart, teaching for me is not about political interests. It is about the teacher–student relation and about the nurturing of learning. Giroux, McLaren, Pennycook and others are themselves teachers, both in university classrooms and through their writings. The reason they teach, and the reason people go to their classes and read their books, is because teaching and learning are inherently valuable processes. One of the things that attracts me to critical pedagogy, on the other hand, is that, as my own personal experience has shown me, many of the pedagogical elements of the critical approach—empowering learners, giving them voice, helping them to see the interestedness of knowledge claims and allowing them to become producers rather than only consumers of knowledge—quite simply constitute excellent pedagogy, from a moral standpoint as well as an educational one.

Let me approach this from another angle. Returning to my own experiences, how was it possible for us to even live in such an oppressive context as that of Communist Poland? It was possible because life is not just about politics, power, and the struggle for social change. People lead rich and fulfilling lives in even the most repressive of regimes, simply because life can never be reduced to political oppression. While a few heroic individuals—the Lech Wałęsas and the Anna Walentynowiczes of the world—took on the political struggle, the rest of us were just trying to live ordinary lives, and for the most part succeeding. In most cases, you do not need to engage in a political struggle to love your family, to enjoy the company of your friends, and to do good and important work, and you do not need complete democracy to engage in meaningful teaching and learning with your students. Democracy, freedom, and social change are all terribly important, but for the great majority of us the real business of life can and must go on regardless, whatever our political context. The alternative view—that until equality among all people is achieved we must devote ourselves above all to the struggle for social change—strikes me as being a bleak prospect indeed, and one that denies the richness and profound humanity of relation, including the teacher–learner relation, as it is played out in whatever circumstances it has found itself.

THE FUNDAMENTAL MORAL DILEMMA
OF POLITICS IN ELT

From a perspective of values, however, rejecting critical pedagogy does not really get us very far, because we are still faced with the same moral problems. I have known several teachers who found the discussions about the political role of the English language that we had in our classes to be

profoundly disturbing, precisely in the sense that they presented moral dilemmas quite independently of whether one embraced critical pedagogy or
not. Indeed, the dilemma ran even deeper: If the spread of English is having, and has had, such a devastating effect on peoples and cultures across
the world, do I even wish to continue to be a part of it? I have not known
teachers who actually gave up teaching for this reason (though I can imagine it happening), but for many teachers, once they develop an awareness
of their own implication in the global processes described by Pennycook
(1994), Phillipson (1992), and others, they often find that, as happened to
me, their view of the world and, more specifically, their own personal and
professional role in it, are radically and permanently changed.

At the same time, not many take up critical pedagogy; most continue
to teach in ways that are not radically different. Why is this? My feeling is that
underlying this whole issue is one of the most profound moral dilemmas of the
ELT profession. This dilemma lies in a moral disjuncture between the broader
political processes described earlier in this chapter and the inherent goodness
that teachers know for certain is an element of their classrooms. For most
teachers, the immediate moral contours of the classroom are clearly delimited:
There is moral worth in developing positive and encouraging relations with
their learners and in acting as a cultural bridge between them and the new culture; there is moral worth in teaching another language; and there is moral
worth in giving these particular individuals access to English, which, other
things being equal, may well improve their lives in any number of potential
ways, whether material, intellectual, or spiritual.

Yet when the teachers look at the political interests vested in English, and at the history of its spread, they cannot deny that it has been and
continues to be a virulent and predacious scourge on the other languages
and cultures of the world. The dilemma dwells in the sheer impossibility of
reconciling these two facts. On the one hand, it is a good thing to teach
English, and the teaching of English is good in several ways that one would
like to think of as universal values. On the other hand, the teaching of English is a bad thing, and it is bad in ways that one would also wish to see as
universal evils.

What is one to do in the face of this dilemma? How does one move
forward knowing both that teaching itself is a moral imperative, and yet
that one is simultaneously implicated in devastating social, cultural and
political processes? I do not have any easy (or even difficult) solutions.
The one thing I know is that each teacher must pick her own path. Critical
pedagogy offers one way forward but, as I pointed out earlier, this is a way

that itself requires a particular set of values and moral choices, and it is not for everyone. It is not an easy puzzle; neither can it be solved by a single decision, but like other moral dynamics it must constantly be addressed with each new group of students and each new teaching and learning situation. I only hope that by showing the problem for what it really is—a moral dilemma that is both highly complex and terribly important— I have helped you to be able to think about it in new and enlightening ways.

QUESTIONS FOR REFLECTION AND DISCUSSION

1. Recall the problem faced by Kay in her work in the Central African Republic. What should she do in this situation? What would *you* do in her place? What values would affect your decision about whether to push for mother-tongue education or whether to concentrate on French?

2. Now look back at the brief description of my work with the Dakota. What, if anything, could or should I have done in this situation? To what extent did I have a right, or a duty, to take further action? Furthermore, what do you think about the question of who was "right" in this context, Angela Wilson or the Tribal Council? What further information would you need in order to decide? Morally speaking, could this conflict be resolved? What other courses of action were open to us?

3. Consider the situation from Bowers and Godfrey's (1985) book presented on p. 62. Are the authors of the book correct to label Yuen-Li's situation a problem? What is your view of the situation presented in this vignette?

4. What is your response to the course of action chosen by Brian Morgan (1997) in his class? How would you have handled the same situation? More generally, how do you decide when your values should override those of your students or the alleged values of their cultures?

5. What do you think about the possibility of using critical pedagogy in EFL settings? What do you think might happen if such an approach were taken in an EFL context with which you are familiar?

6. Consider your own teaching situation. What political forces act on it? Who gets to choose what books are used, what cur-

riculum is selected, or how examinations are organized? What values are brought to bear in these decisions?

7. The spread of English in the world has been widely documented. What is your view of this process? What values does the spread of English carry with it—for example, in the teaching context in which you work?

The Morality of Testing and Assessment

THE MORALITY OF ASSESSMENT

I start this chapter with a very simple story about tests told to me by Wen-Hsing, a former student of mine who now teaches at a secondary school back home in Taiwan. Wen-Hsing recently sent me an e-mail about what happened when she and her colleagues were grading the English language component of an entrance exam:

> One section of the English test was: "According to the picture, answer the following five questions." It was a picture of a classroom, where there is a teacher standing and six students seated. It looked like two of the students were talking to each other and the teacher was not happy about it. One of the five questions was "Why is the teacher angry? The teacher is angry because students are __." This blank only allowed one word and the "standard" answer, according to the test-giver, was "talking."
>
> When we were grading the answer sheet, we found there were a variety of answers and some of them that seemed possible were "playing," "noisy," "bad." Thus, we voted to decide if we would accept these answers. Interestingly, "noisy" and "bad" were accepted but "playing" was rejected. The reason of the majority was that we could not tell from the picture whether these two students were playing or not. Well then, I asked them, "Can you tell from the picture that these two are bad?" The answer I got was "We all agreed not to include 'playing' in the answers. If we reached an agreement, it is fine."
>
> Although I would like to give students whose answer was "playing" credit, I couldn't do it and I graded those answer sheets the way I was told to do.
>
> This case was not unique. It happened every time I graded in the entrance exam. I don't know why some possible answers

were accepted but some were not. I think it is good to have students answer questions according to the picture they see, but is it necessary to restrict the number of answers? You know what, I always felt "not so good" after grading because there was always one or two answers that would arise dispute.

The problems faced by Wen-Hsing and her colleagues reveal the profoundly moral nature of assessment in language teaching. These Taiwanese teachers are striving to adjudicate which knowledge is sanctioned and which is not; their deliberations involve drawing lines in the sand where there are few if any objective criteria unambiguously separating right from wrong. Yet the consequences of their decisions will be visited on the children of their classes and, over time, will become part of each child's permanent record.

Of course, one could argue that the item in question is simply badly designed and that what is needed is just a better test composed of less ambiguous questions. Yet I believe that anyone who has tried to write a test, whether a professional test designer or a classroom teacher, will recognize the difficulties the Taiwanese teachers face. With such a phenomenally complex thing as a language, there are limitless problems that arise in determining ways of testing students' knowledge; the more complicated and interesting that knowledge becomes, the harder it is to test (Bachman, 2000). Furthermore, those who are most adept at writing test items—professional testers—are also those farthest removed from the classroom, and thus they lack information about what has been covered in class by particular groups of students. All of us are obliged to make do with faulty tools in the work of evaluating students.

In this chapter I explore the moral dynamics underlying various aspects of testing and evaluation. During the discussion, I raise many complex moral questions both about traditional forms of evaluation such as standardized tests and examinations, and about alternative approaches to assessment such as portfolios. I argue, however, that two profound moral paradoxes underlie the entire realm of language testing and assessment.

Two Paradoxes of Values in Assessment

The first paradox is that of test subjectivity. On the one hand, testers place great emphasis on the goal of objectivity in testing. This seems, by and large, a worthy goal. Yet testing, more than any other aspect of teaching, is value laden—and, as we have seen, values are inherently subjective in nature (Gipps & Murphy, 1994). The selection of what to test, how it will be tested, and how scores are to be interpreted are all acts that require human judgment; that is, they are subjective acts. The preceding example of Wen-Hsing and her colleagues is a miniature example of this process. It follows quite naturally that the process of assigning and grading a test or other work by a student—that is, the process of *evaluation*—is precisely that: a process of placing a *value* on the head of each individual student. If this is not a moral act, nothing is. Furthermore, while subjectivity is on the whole not a desirable quality, flexibility is; and flexibility in testing—accepting the word *playing* in Wen-Hsing's test, for example, when the official key allows only *talking*—can be achieved only through the subjective decision making of a particular teacher with particular students who happen to produce these answers (once again, we find ourselves back at the critical place of the teacher–student relation).

The second paradox, which intermeshes with and compounds the first, is what I shall refer to as *the paradox of the necessary evil*. On the one hand, tests and other forms of assessment are undesirable, and a great many teachers dislike them. Not only are they unreliable and inherently disposed to unfairness, as described earlier, but they are also stressful on students (and, in different ways, on teachers, too), and they take precious time and attention from what most of us see as the real purpose of education: learning. Tests are often designed more from the point of view of administrative convenience than that of the students' needs. Furthermore, there is an ever-present political aspect to testing that often takes over: The already unhealthy societal preoccupation with testing magnifies these problems to the point where the processes and goals of education are seriously undermined.

On the other hand, however, most teachers would also recognize that some form of evaluation, though it may not be pleasant, is in fact essential not just for the convenience of the teacher or the school but for the learners themselves. Learners, and their teachers, need to have a sense of how well they are doing: of their progress, of how their work measures up to expectations, maybe even of how they stand in relation to their peers. Without this information, they can feel lost and adrift. Furthermore, many teachers (myself included) like to be able to have some way of rewarding outstanding work and giving due recognition to those who perform particularly well. Thus, while evaluation is undesirable for moral reasons, it is at the same time necessary, also for moral reasons; it is a necessary evil.

These, then, are the two fundamental paradoxes with which we enter the discussion of values and assessment in language teaching: the first is the dynamic of objectivity and subjectivity in testing; the second is the simultaneous desirability and undesirability of assessment.

The Moral Contours of Assessment

These two paradoxes, profound and central as they are, do not exhaust the moral contours of assessment procedures. Assessment—any form of assessment—is moral in a number of ways. First and foremost, assessment is moral because, as I mentioned earlier, it quite literally places a value on each individual student. This value is usually given either as a percentage or some other fraction, a score, or a letter grade. In the colossal majority of cases, the student falls short of mathematical "perfection."

Assessment is also moral in that most forms of assessment in some way measure one student against another—that is, they assign not just an absolute value but also a relative value. Here issues of justice creep in: There is a delicate balance between treating everyone equally and rewarding those who do better, whether through hard work, innate ability, or a combination of these (an important issue to which I return a bit later).

Furthermore, assessment is moral because it often has serious real-world consequences for learners. The grades we give our students, and the scores they obtain on standardized tests, often have huge significance in their lives: Because of these scores and grades, they get or do not get accepted into programs, they are or are not given scholarships and funds, they are or are not promoted, are or are not given a raise, and so on. (Remember the consequences faced by Peter's Palestinian student in the story told at the beginning of chap. 1.) Our decisions form the direct or indirect sources of these assessments and thus carry great moral weight, because we have to be sure (as in fact we rarely can be) that the aforementioned kinds of decisions are just and fair, that the "best" candidates (once again a moral expression) have in fact been successful.

Last, assessment is also moral because, like everything else in teaching, it is conducted in complex and morally ambiguous real-world contexts, and to be understood properly it cannot be divorced from those contexts or seen to be merely about the learning of languages. The dilemma faced by Peter in chapter 1 is an example of the way in which the world beyond the language classroom can impinge hugely on our decision making in student evaluation: Here, the political realities of life outside class made an apparently straightforward evaluation of the student's abilities horribly complex in moral terms. The decision that Peter made had, of course, no impact on that student's knowledge of English. My point is precisely that sometimes, whether we like it or not, a student's abilities are not the only thing that needs to be taken into consideration.

Let me share an example parallel with that of Peter. A friend of mine, Alison, recently took a junior faculty position in the French department of a well-known private university. She had a student who wished to take a minor in French; to do so, he needed a B minimum in his language classes. Yet the student was lazy and rather arrogant and signally failed to do work at a level that would allow him to receive a B. Alison gave him a lower grade. She was called to the dean, who quietly explained to Alison that this student's parents had donated millions of dollars to the university and that the university was counting on further donations. Like Peter, Alison reluctantly changed the grade she had awarded. I tell this story not to condemn Alison, but quite the opposite—to show how complicated the real world of evaluating students can be. As with Peter, the final grade Alison gave did not in the least represent some reassessment of the student but was a result of external factors; nevertheless, the final grade is what counts in the real world.[1]

Neither do the moral contours of evaluation end here. An additional moral dilemma is the constant and unresolved (indeed, unresolvable) dynamic between formative and summative functions of assessment. Assessment specialists commonly draw a distinction between *formative* assessment—that is, assessment designed to indicate to a student how he or she is doing—with *summative* assessment, which measures final achievement in a course or program (Rea-Dickins & Gardner, 2000; Torrance & Pryor, 1998). Yet in reality the distinction is not clear. Certain summative forms of evaluation take on a formative role: For example, when I received what is known as an Upper Second bachelor's degree from my university in England—a summative qualification—I also took this as a formative indication that, without a first-class degree, I had no business returning to postgraduate education. It took me some time to revise my interpretation and enter a doctoral program.

Conversely—and, I believe, more commonly—grades or marks that are meant to have a formative role take on certain summative qualities. For example, many kinds of evaluation, such as quizzes and midterms, are intended to let students know how they are doing. Yet often scores from these sources also factor into final grades; thus, the evaluation is also summative in that it forms part of the summative grade. Moreover, even when this is not the case,

---

[1]Julian Edge has pointed out to me that there are other moral aspects to this story, too. The parents' desire to look after their son's interests is also morally justifiable, as are the potential benefits from the expected donations to many other students at the university, including some whom scholarship money would allow to participate in otherwise prohibitively expensive programs.

formative evaluations *look* like summative ones; they often come in the form of scores on tests in which there is little in the way of feedback. I suggest that this resemblance leads learners to see the teacher as a judge rather than as a teacher, once again affecting the teacher–student relation.

Last, the truly dilemmatic nature of approaches to assessment is underscored by the fact that, in light of the paradox of the necessary evil, a decision not to use any form of assessment at all is also a moral act. By choosing not to give any exams or other methods of assessment, a teacher is of course relieving students of the stress and all the attendant vagaries of determining what counts as knowledge. However, such a teacher is also sending other moral messages to her students. Many students might believe that this decision reflects an underlying indifference to what the students learn and hence to them as people; that is, once again it will affect the teacher–student relation. Students who would normally strive to excel will have a reduced motivation to do so—in fact, only those students truly engaged in the subject matter are likely to remain unaffected and, as most teachers would agree, such students are rarely in the majority (Milton, Pollio, & Eison, 1986). Furthermore, regardless of the theoretical arguments, exams can function to help students distinguish important from less important aspects of what they cover; the absence of exams makes such distinctions much harder.

In many ways, then, the moral landscape of assessment is complex and difficult terrain. Both the inner workings of assessment procedures and their broader sociopolitical context are such that questions of assessment are always also questions of values. These values, in turn, are never straightforward but always fraught with conflict.

VALUES AND CLASSROOM ASSESSMENT

In this section I focus on forms of assessment that are designed, administered, and evaluated by teachers themselves. Although, as I mentioned earlier, I believe that all forms of assessment have moral meaning, assessments by teachers of their own students carry particular kinds of moral significance.

Assessment and the Teacher–Student Relation

However we evaluate our students, when we come to do so we are always and inevitably faced with an insurmountable moral problem. In all that I have read on testing and teaching, I have nowhere seen it better expressed than by Nel Noddings (1984). In the following passage she begins by reaffirming the paramount importance of the teacher–student relation:

> Teaching involves two persons in a special relationship. Usually, there is a fairly well-defined "something" in which the two engage, but this is not always true. Sometimes teacher and student just explore. They explore something, of course, but this something is not always prespecified; nor need it remain constant or, for that matter, even lead somewhere definite. The essence is in the relationship. In the relationship, the teacher has become a duality: she shares the view of the objects under study with the student. Then suddenly, grindingly, she must wrench herself from the relationship and make her student into an object of scrutiny. (p. 195)

This "grinding" quality of assessment practices is an unavoidable consequence of the teacher–student relation. If we were merely technicians conveying information, there would be no moral dimension to assessment. However, we are not, and this dimension not only exists but is of central importance in our approach to assessment. As teachers, we wish to be supportive—to push our students, yes, but to do so in ways that make them feel challenged yet also free to fail without consequences. At the same time, the need to evaluate—which, as I argued in the preceding section, is also a moral imperative—not only does not promote that kind of relation but actively works against it.

It is important to point out that this moral dilemma does not go away when teachers do not have control over the testing practices used in their classrooms. They still participate in the processes of evaluation; from the point of view of the teacher–student relation, the net result is the same: the "grinding" sensation described by Noddings. The only difference is that the teacher has not had a voice in determining what material counts as knowledge for the purposes of the examination.

In the previous section, I mentioned several ways in which assessment procedures cannot help but influence the teacher–student relation. One other crucial aspect of this influence must be mentioned here: the question of *trust*. Implicit in a great many aspects of testing is a lack of trust toward students: Everything from seating patterns to the meticulously controlled matter of test security are established in ways that assume a default tendency to cheat on their part. Trust, in turn, is an implicit belief in the fundamental goodness of the other. Absence of trust, by the same token, indicates a lack of a belief in the other's basic goodness. In our mechanisms of control we are passing moral judgment on our learners.

Assessing Knowledge of Language

A central question in the assessment of language learning—possibly the most important of all—is: What does it mean to know a language? Anyone designing any kind of evaluation has to answer this question; yet to do so is already to begin to make morally significant judgments. Is language knowing vocabulary? Being able to recite grammar rules? To buy an airplane ticket? To translate sentences? To write a persuasive essay? In choosing between these and a thousand other options, we are making choices that will have significant effects on our students and their performance. Consider the relatively simple case of Wen-Hsing mentioned earlier, where choices of what is and is not acceptable, reached by group consensus, left students who had given grammatically acceptable answers with a worse score. Furthermore, the fact of the matter is that our choices themselves are largely based on what I have called faith, that is, our beliefs about the nature of language, learning language and knowing language that are grounded only partly in logic and can never be fully confirmed or disproved (see chap. 1). Knowing a language is a phenomenally complicated thing; in determining how to test that knowledge we are forced to make choices that oversimplify the picture (McNamara, 1996). Our choices, furthermore, have demonstrable consequences for students. Ania, my elder daughter, who is bilingual in English and Polish, returned to Poland for some of her high school education. In one of her English classes she failed a major exam because she did not "know" the grammar of English and so was unable to understand instructions such as: "Convert the following sentences into the present perfect tense," even though she was able to *use* such structures with nativelike ability in her speech. Her teachers had chosen to define knowledge of English as knowledge of grammatical terminology rather than the actual ability to speak the language (which for Ania would not have been a problem). Of course, we have some general guidelines—it is good pedagogical practice, for example, to test what has been covered in class and not what has not (Genesee & Upshur, 1996; Herman, Aschbacher, & Winters, 1992)—but this merely begs the question of what should be taught in class.

The business of testing is even more complicated because there is only ever an indirect relation between our notion of what it is to know a language and the form of evaluation we devise. Even if we believe that language learning is a matter of vocabulary only, we have to select certain lexical items to be included in the test and exclude others. The situation is, of course, infinitely more complex if we have a more sophisticated understanding of knowledge of language, including areas such as pragmatics and discourse. In parallel fashion, there is only ever an indirect relationship between a student's performance in a test and her actual knowledge of the language, whether for reasons of nerves or having a good day or bad day, or from the universally acknowledged slippage between competence and performance. All of these factors mean that to devise a test and to assign scores or grades to those who take it is to sail out onto very dark and deep moral waters indeed.

Last, another fundamental conundrum is that neither language nor competence in language is naturally measurable. If we are judging how high a person can jump, we can pretty much agree on who jumps higher than others: Height is simple to measure. It is not at all clear, however, how we can objectively measure how well someone speaks another language. We find ourselves resorting to subjective terms such as fluent, hesitant, and difficulty (Richard-Amato, 1996, pp. 99–100), which require constant interpretation, and once more, the more sophisticated our attempts at measurement become, the harder they are to pull together into a cohesive overall assessment. The fundamental *immeasurability* of language competence lends a further moral dimension to our work in language assessment; the decisions we are forced to make about how competence will be assessed are always subjective and thus can only be rooted in our beliefs about what is right and good, beliefs which, we must always acknowledge, could be mistaken.

Assessment Beyond Language

The value-laden nature of assessment, moreover, goes far beyond the simple matter of how to measure language ability. There are also crucial educational considerations to take into account.

A central moral dilemma for many teachers, for example, at least in this country, is the extent to which they should reward effort, or ability, or achievement. Up until this point, I have been assuming that evaluation is intended to measure the student's ability in English. But in much ESL teaching in the United States and certain other countries, great emphasis is placed on a student's engagement in, or commitment to, her work. It is thought important to reward effort—the time and energy devoted to an assignment, rather than merely the quality of the finished product, or the willingness to participate in classroom discussion rather than the grammatical correctness of the contributions or the value of their substance. In this there is very clearly an issue of moral judgment: In rewarding "good" behavior, we are standing in judgment over the learner; we are adjudicating "good" and "bad" ways to be as well as knowledge of the subject matter. There is a strong component of moral education in the old-fashioned sense, of instilling and reinforcing desirable behaviors, habits, and attitudes in our students (Jackson, Boostrom & Hansen, 1993). At the same time, another aspect of the moral dimension of power emerges, as we punish those who do not behave in approved ways, for example, giving lower grades to students who do not willingly take part in classroom activities, fail to turn in journals or other written work on time, and so on. What function does this punishment serve? As a warning for the future? As a sign to others? In any case, surely its consequences are not restricted to the moment in which a bad grade is given and received.

Let me share an example of the complex issues at play here. For her doctoral dissertation, Ewald (2001) interviewed university-level students and teachers of Spanish about their attitudes toward group work. One teacher she spoke to, Gonzalo, explained that he graded students on their contributions to small-group work. The students to whom Ewald spoke, however, felt that this was an unfair practice, pointing out that although they accept the usefulness of small-group work, for some students participation in such groups is rendered difficult for nonlinguistic reasons such as shyness.

Ewald (2001, p. 166) reported that Gonzalo's practice is grounded in a belief that evaluation of this aspect of their work in class will motivate students to participate more and help them to see the value of small-group work (and we know that in language classes, the more you speak, the more you learn). He might also have wished to be able to reward the students who contribute more willingly. Yet, as the students' reaction shows, this practice brings with it several moral dilemmas. First, there is the question of the extent to which personality traits such as shyness should affect one's grade. Second, Ewald pointed out that the students were already aware of the expectation of participation and did not need to be reminded of it. This becomes a matter of trust (p. 167): That is, the practice of evaluating contributions to group work carries with it the implication that without the pressure of the evaluation students cannot be trusted to participate of their own accord. I would also point out a third issue of measurement: the problem of how to assign scores fairly to something as complex as participation in a small group.

The practice of rewarding hard work as well as "objectively" measured ability gives rise to its own moral dilemmas. What do we do with those students who work terribly hard and yet simply do not have the wherewithal to do A-grade work? Conversely, what do we do with the bright but disaffected students who are able to speak fluently and write expressively yet will not take part in classroom dialogue and do the minimum to scrape by in their written work? Once, many years ago (when I still gave exams), in an undergraduate class on second language acquisition I had a student who barely came to class at all yet turned up for the midterm exam and did tolerably well. What is one to do in such a situation? What was *I* to do? At one level, the student had done what she was supposed to: She had learned the material the course covered. At another level, she had flouted the (in this case unwritten) rules of engagement of the academy, which state that good students are expected to do the things that good students do: come to class, take part in discussions, show interest, and so on.

A related issue is whether one aims to measure ability or achievement. Often I have had students who come to the class knowing very little about the matter at hand and who learn a lot during the class. Do these students deserve a better grade than those who knew a great deal more at the beginning yet at the end may still know more than their colleagues?

Such questions raise the specter of our purpose in teaching in the first place. If indeed we aim merely to transmit information or knowledge, then we should reward the student who has, or has acquired, more information or knowledge. However, throughout this book I have been arguing that teaching cannot and should not be reduced to the transfer of information. It is primarily about the moral relation between teacher and student. This said, however, the teacher, as one-caring (Noddings, 1984), is in a different position than the student, the cared-for. What is the moral responsibility of the latter toward the former? Noddings (1984) suggested that while the teacher's responsibility is greater, there is still a need for reciprocity (pp. 69–74). Yet to what extent is it our responsibility to judge the student on matters of character or innate ability? I argued in chapter 3 that there is an element of moral education in adult ESL settings. Yet what of other contexts? How far do our duties go beyond teaching the language and into the territory of character formation?

An additional point is the moral dilemma that arises from the fact that students have different levels of ability. The questions I have just raised—whether students should be rewarded for effort or for achievement and whether progress is as important as final achievement—cannot really be answered without referring to differing levels of aptitude. Some students, for whatever reason, are simply good at languages; others, to use a Polish expression, are anti-talents when it comes to language learning. In a sense, this is a matter of "moral luck" (Statman, 1993): Some people are "born better" in one regard or another. At college, my friend Brett would regularly infuriate me by finishing his French essays in a scrawl as we were walking to class together; he invariably got an A. I think most of us have known other Bretts, whether as friends or students of ours. Should he and his kind be rewarded for simply being better and faster? It seems to me that try as we might to evaluate students on language alone, we cannot help but take other, morally charged circumstances into consideration; the question is, are we aware of this? If so, have we thought through the moral consequences of our decision?

Who Is a Good Student?

Throughout this discussion I have deliberately been using the words *good* and *bad*. This whole discussion ultimately, revolves around a fundamental ambiguity inherent in the phrase *good student* (Amirault, 1995). On the one hand, a good student is one who does well: learns, passes tests and exams, and so on. These qualities and achievements are moral in nature the way that education in general is moral in nature. It is good to learn, to know more, to have more skills and abilities. Yet even here there is ambiguity. What exactly does it mean to do well, to succeed? Such questions once again go to the heart of our purpose in teaching. In an adult literacy class, for example, is a student successful if he reads a newspaper article? Or passes his GED (the high school equivalency examination)? Or if he gets a job? We might also ask: What of the student who learns well but does not pass the exam? Or what of the EFL student who gets only a C in English yet is promptly hired to teach English in an elementary school? (I have known such teachers myself.)

Furthermore, there is a social notion of the "good" student that is also moral in nature, yet in a different way. This notion of the "good student" takes *good* to mean obedient, pleasant, willing, hard working, conscientious, persistent—all of which, of course, are also morally desirable characteristics, and which, other things being equal, equip students better to benefit from their education. Yet this meaning of "good student" cannot always be reconciled with that mentioned in the preceding paragraph: Some students work hard and are pleasant but do not properly grasp the subject matter; others are sullen and lazy yet smart. What do we—what do *you*—mean when you use the expression "She's a good student"? Which of these meanings is more important to you, and to the student concerned? Which meanings are reflected in the system of values underlying the forms of assessment you use?

It is important to emphasize the symbiotic relationship between the moral messages sent by our assessment practices and our notions of what it is to be a good student. It is through whatever assessment practices we use that the identity of good or bad student is encoded in schools; conversely, our idea of the good student affects the kinds of assessment we select. In either case, multiple powerful and complex moral meanings are to be found in the kinds of tests and other forms of evaluation that we use in our classrooms.

VALUES AND STANDARDIZED TESTING: THE MORALITY OF THE TEST OF ENGLISH AS A FOREIGN LANGUAGE (TOEFL)

Everything I wrote earlier about the value-laden nature of assessment practices—that they are oriented to product rather than process, that they favor certain candidates over others, that they are used for administrative convenience rather than serving the needs of the learners—applies in spades in the case of standardized tests such as the TOEFL.

Yet the TOEFL and its ilk also raise an additional set of moral concerns and dilemmas. Elana Shohamy (1998), one of the first people to raise questions about the "ethical" dimensions of language testing, described the widespread use of standardized tests to promote bureaucratic and political agendas. She identified three ethical consequences of such uses of tests:

1. The "institutionalized knowledge" (p. 339) that tests canonize is "narrow, simplistic and often different from experts' knowledge" (p. 339). The kind of knowledge tested, which often involves single-word answers in multiple-choice formats, "overlooks the complexities of subject matter and is unmeaningful for repair" (p. 339).
2. A "parallel system" (p. 340) is created whereby stated policy is at odds with the "organizational aspirations" reflected in the tests. Shohamy gave the example of Israel, where "both Hebrew and Arabic are official languages, yet, on the high school entrance exam Arabs are tested in Hebrew, while Hebrew speakers are not tested in Arabic" (p. 340).
3. Ethical problems arise when "the test becomes a means through which the policy makers communicate priorities to the system" (p. 340). Shohamy sees this as "undemocratic and unethical" (p. 340) because those affected by the test—the students who take it and the teachers who teach them—have no say in the design and implementation of the test.

This last point deserves further consideration. I would argue that the most serious moral concerns with such tests arise from their impersonal nature. As Shohamy (1998) pointed out, the people affected by the test have no say in its creation; through such procedures it is much easier to maintain the myth of the objective test, because the people who create the questions and assess performance are nowhere around—unlike with a teacher or school department, to which students usually have some kind of access. This, combined with the strict and ritualistic way in which standardized tests are conducted, gives the knowledge they enshrine a solemn, almost sacred significance. The political, "interested" nature of knowledge featured in chapter 3 is a powerful component here too. I argue that there is deep moral meaning in such an approach to knowledge: By reducing learners to recipients of knowledge rather than creators of it, one is also reducing their capacity for moral agency.

There is also a question of honesty here. Because of the veil of objectivity behind which they hide, standardized tests ride roughshod over the unavoidable difficulties of matching score with actual ability. The final score is presented (and in the overwhelming majority of cases is also treated) as an objective measure: The uncertainties and ambiguities that attend test development, and the myriad psychological factors that affect a candidate's performance on a given day, are invisible.

Furthermore, because of the physical and administrative distance between the testers and those tested, appeals are difficult, if not impossible. A teacher might possibly be inclined to be lenient on a student whose grandfather died a few days before the exam, or to give a student who has difficulty writing an extra minute or two at the end of a test. A standardized test can offer neither of these possibilities or anything like them. What is missing here is relation: The human relation between tester and testee, which exists when teachers prepare tests, and which informed the whole of the previous section, is entirely absent in the standardized test. By this account, the moral contours of the test are quite different. The educational process is suddenly deprived of its deepest and most meaningful component. This feature is underlined even more in the current shift to computerized testing in the TOEFL and many other common tests.

The impersonal nature of such tests, and the impossibility of our understanding the human dimension of the test-taking experience of any specific individual, makes it very difficult for the consumers of test score information to know how to interpret them. As language professionals, we know the complexities I have been discussing here; as a result, reading the scores is very much a matter of interpretation rather than a simple acknowledgment of a score. Just 2 days ago I was reviewing some late admissions for our own master's and doctoral programs. One candidate from a western European country had an English mother, and her entire application confirmed her own categorization of herself as "virtually bilingual," yet her TOEFL score was a mere 597, which, the computer-generated form from the university's Office of International Admissions told us, indicated that she "may need supplementary English training." A doctoral candidate from an African country in which English is widely spoken had attended an English-language university for his undergraduate and master's degrees and had sterling references and published academic work, yet his scores on the TOEFL and Graduate Record Examination were both abysmally low. What should we do in such situations? Both candidates were admitted, but in each case the test scores complicated the decision rather than making it easier; in the case of scores on the Graduate Record Examination, for example, we are required by the university's graduate school to obtain an official exception for any candidate who does not score the required minimum in this test.

Another moral paradox is the disjuncture between testing and current pedagogical practice in language teaching (Hamp-Lyons, 1998). The communicative model that, in various forms, is widely used across the world encourages students to engage in meaningful interaction using whatever linguistic means they have at their disposal; it specifically downplays the importance of grammatical accuracy over communicative effectiveness. Although some tests have made more or less successful attempts to integrate communicative competence in their evaluations of students (the Cambridge suite of examinations and the ACTFL's [American Council for the Teaching of Foreign Languages] proficiency guidelines for foreign languages [Byrnes & Canale, 1987] come to mind; see also Powers, Schedl, & Wilson, 1999), the TOEFL has notably lagged behind in this regard, and many other tests still focus narrowly on grammar and vocabulary.[2]

One consequence of this disjuncture is the so-called *washback effect*: the ways in which test format affects teaching. The theory behind the TOEFL, like any test of its kind, is that it is a snapshot of a candidate's language ability at a given moment in time; thus, it should not be possible to improve one's performance other than by more study of the language. In reality, of course, TOEFL preparation courses and programs abound. Liz Hamp-Lyons (1998) offered a very thoughtful analysis of some of the ethical (what I would call moral) issues that arise from the "powerful" (p. 331) washback effect of such an influential test as the TOEFL. Drawing on the

---

[2]Of course, I am sidestepping the fact that with a so-called communicative test it is still necessary to define what knowledge of language is and to ignore the fact that an examination virtually by definition cannot involve genuine communication and therefore will always be only an indirect and artificial indication of the candidate's "true" ability, however *ability* is defined.

work of Mehrens and Kaminsky (1989) and Popham (1991), Hamp-Lyons posed the question of what constitutes "ethical test preparation" (p. 334) and argued that existing materials (and hence a great deal of existing test preparation programs across the world) are "educationally indefensible (boosting scores without mastery) and of dubious ethicality (coaching merely for score gain)" (p. 334). She went on to ask a series of provocative and important questions, all of which have a strong moral dimension:

> Can a test be blamed for the ways in which some teachers teach towards it? […] Or is it the fault of the students who demand a certain kind of teaching? […] Is it perhaps the fault of the teaching institutions, which do not provide any kind of teacher training in TOEFL preparation? […] Or is training in teaching test preparation the responsibility of the textbook writers and publishers? (p. 335)

Hamp-Lyons' (1998) questions remind me of the social nature of morality. The point of her questions, as I understand them, is not to apportion ultimate blame ("yes, it's the students' fault") but to point up the fact that adjudicating on moral issues is a highly complex process in which many individuals and institutions have a stake. Standardized tests are social phenomena par excellence; any consideration of their moral significance must begin from this starting point.

For example, much as I loathe the whole business of tests, when it comes to my own students I can understand why they would want to have extra preparation. Although at one level such an approach demolishes both the illusion of the snapshot-of-ability principle and the principle of equality and fairness, on the other hand, the moral importance of relation creeps in. It is never the case, and I would argue that it never should be, that a teacher's own students are not more important than some other students in another state or country. We want the best for our own students, even if in general moral terms it could give them an "unfair" advantage. This is a classic instance of the way in which individual circumstances and specific relations color our approach to moral dilemmas.

This brings me to a final point, which Noddings (1984) raised in her discussion of assessment. Contrary to received wisdom regarding the preferability of local, teacher-developed forms of assessment over mass standardized testing, Noddings wrote that she is "convinced … that grading—summative evaluation of any kind—should not be done by teachers. If it must be done, it should be done by external examiners, persons hired to look at students as objects. Then teacher and students would be recognized as together in the battle against ignorance" (p. 195).

Despite my instinctive and growing distaste for standardized tests of all kinds, I find Noddings' argument curiously persuasive because, like her, I believe that our prime duty as teachers is to focus on the learning of our own students. Turning the problem of evaluation over to outsiders moves it from the immediate, local teacher–student relation, and spares that relation the "grinding" experience mentioned earlier in which the teacher switches caps from advocate to judge. Noddings' (1984) suggestion does not justify indiscriminate use of testing and it does not offer any justification of current testing practices or excuse test makers from an obligation to continually rethink the format and nature of their tests. It does, however, remind us that we are dealing with issues of immense moral complexity, in which unequivocal good and bad, right and wrong, are terribly hard to pin down.

VALUES AND ALTERNATIVE ASSESSMENT

Over the last 20 years or so, a significantly different approach to assessment has been developed (Genesee & Upshur, 1996; Herman et al., 1992; A. Katz, 2000; O'Malley & Valdez Pierce, 1996; Torrance, 1995). *Alternative assessment*, as it is generally known (the term *authentic assessment* is also used), takes as its starting point a vigorous critique of conventionally used forms of assessment such as multiple-choice tests. The case against traditional assessment includes many of the arguments I have already mentioned in this chapter: that these forms of assessment test the wrong kinds of knowledge, appealing to memorization and simplistic knowing of facts rather than deeper understanding; that they are designed with administrative convenience in mind rather than being grounded in the best interests of the students; that they are unnecessarily stressful; and that they aim to catch students out with what they do not know rather than allowing them to show what they do. In place of such tests, alternative assessment offers various options, including portfolio assessment, "kidwatching" (Goodman, 1985) and other forms of continual assessment, teacher–student learning contracts, and a range of other ideas.

Before I continue this discussion I would like to state for the record that I find the case against traditional assessment rather convincing. I have not given an exam in more than 7 years; I do all of my assessment by alternative methods, including portfolios, journals, written assignments, and so on. I practice this both in my teacher education classes and my ESL teaching. Nevertheless, my point here is that even if one agrees that these methods are superior, they are still value laden, and they still involve complex moral issues and moral dilemmas. In this section I explore the moral underpinnings of alternative approaches to assessment. I center the discussion around a series of moral dilemmas that inhere in the processes of instituting and maintaining portfolio assessment in the language classroom (Genesee & Upshur, 1996). Many other approaches are possible in alternative assessment, but the portfolio is probably the best known of its techniques. In addition, such a focus allows me to be more concrete in my discussion.

A *portfolio* is an organized collection of different pieces of work by a student that is presented in lieu of a traditional examination for the purposes of assessment. Portfolios are often thematic but loosely structured; their function is to demonstrate both the range and the quality of a student's work (Cole, Ryan, & Kick, 1995; De Fina, 1992; Genesee & Upshur, 1996).

Several important features of the portfolio contrast with aspects of traditional assessment mentioned earlier. First, the portfolio is designed to show what the student can do and does know as opposed to what he or she cannot do and does not know. For this reason, an important element in the process of compiling a portfolio is that the student be able to choose which pieces of work are included and which are not. Second, portfolios are intended to give a richer picture of the student's abilities and understanding than can be gleaned from one-word multiple-choice answers; thus, portfolios often focus on more extended, contextualized pieces of work such as written essays. Third, in contrast with traditional tests, which provide at best only a snapshot in time of the learner's competence, portfolios aim to show the growth of that competence; to this end, they often include drafts of papers along with the final versions, or a series of written pieces that show improvement over time. Last, because a portfolio is assembled over the period of a semester or a term (or longer), the stressful practice of cramming all one knows into a single 2-hr exam at the end of the course is avoided.

I truly believe that portfolios represent a huge improvement over traditional forms of assessment; I use them myself, and there is growing evidence that they constitute an effective assessment tool (Torrance, 1995). Nevertheless, as I mentioned earlier, portfolios are by no means exempt from the complex moral dilemmas that inform other kinds of evaluation. In the remainder of this section I outline the principal moral issues that the use of portfolios entails.

First, we must acknowledge that, for many students, it is considerably easier to memorize a few vocabulary items and grammar structures than to compile a portfolio; that is, traditional forms of assessment are often easier on certain students. In deciding whether to institute portfolio assessment, then, we face the moral decision of whether this innovation truly serves the best interests of the students. Can we be sure that the gains from the portfolio are worth the effort required of our students (and ourselves)? Related to this are what are sometimes termed *ecological considerations*: How does the portfolio relate to the broader curriculum and the educational and social system in which students are situated? In Japan, for example, many students need English primarily to pass grammar-oriented tests that in turn will allow them to enter a good college; in such cases, assessment by portfolio, while in principle justifiable, may not in practice be defensible if the students' needs and goals are factored into the equation. Such decisions involve moral considerations of what is right and good for particular students in particular sociopolitical, cultural, and educational contexts.

Even in contexts where portfolios might be more appropriate—for example, U. S. academic English programs—there is often considerable resistance from the learners themselves. Although I certainly do not believe that such resistance represents an absolute impediment to change, I also believe that we have a moral responsibility to take our learners' viewpoints seriously. This is part of the dialogue that forms the foundation of the teacher–student relation. Furthermore, for education to take place, we cannot simply bemoan the fact that our students are not where we would like them to be. All true education takes the students where they are and leads them from there. This notion has been echoed by authors as diverse as Nel Noddings (1984) and Paulo Freire (1972).

Another aspect of the teacher–student relation that arises here is that of responsibility. Though this varies from case to case, use of portfolios always involves a considerable shift of responsibility (for selecting material, ordering it, and presenting it) from the teacher to the student. Of course, practical problems often arise in such circumstances. Some students fail to take on this responsibility, whether out of rebellion, inertia, or some other reason. Yet underlying these practical matters is one of the fundamental moral paradoxes of our profession. On the one hand, the field as a whole supports student autonomy, responsibility, and empowerment; we teachers sometimes question whether there is even such a thing as "teaching," and we portray ourselves rather as "people who help others to learn." Yet on the other hand, we know both intellectually and personally that there *is* such a thing as teaching, and that there are considerably better and considerably worse ways of doing it, and we take personal responsibility for the successes and failures of our learners. It is terribly difficult to figure out where the responsibility of the teacher ends and that of the learner begins. The notion of the teacher–student relation to some extent addresses this conundrum, suggesting that it is neither one nor the other, but the relation between them that is the key factor. Yet at the end of the (school) day each of us teachers is an individual, and each of us wonders about our own agency, its moral obligations and moral limits. The practice of portfolio assessment is one attempt to shift the balance of this dynamic in one particular direction, but the underlying dynamic remains.

The last moral dilemma I examine in relation to student portfolios is this: How exactly are we to evaluate them? It is here that the paradox of subjectivity in testing comes back to haunt us, along with Noddings' (1984) problem of the moral dissonance that occurs when teachers become evaluators. The fact is that although the other desirable characteristics of portfolios—student choice, lack of stress, a capacity for capturing both deeper understanding and development over time—remain in place, many of the moral dilemmas attendant on traditional testing are still present. How is student work to be graded? As before, do we reward progress over time, or final ability, or hard work, or all three? In what combinations? Also as before, though the evidence in portfolios is considerably richer than that in multiple-choice tests, it is still only indirect evidence, and still must be filtered through the interpretive understanding of the teacher.

Moreover, the apparent flexibility of the portfolio also conceals another uncomfortable moral dynamic: The greater the freedom and flexibility of the design of the portfolio, the harder it is for the teacher to evaluate it. If I allow one student to write an essay for one component, and another student to write a poem for the same assignment, how can the two be compared? Furthermore, when it comes to grading, I face the same problems mentioned earlier. If I give a student extra leeway for a poorly done assignment handed in at a difficult personal time for that student, am I using or abusing the special relation I have with him and with other students? Conversely, how can I grade evenly and yet also reward outstanding work that I believe deserves special recognition? To what extent is subjectivity an advantage, and how can I know when it becomes a hindrance? In some teaching situations, teachers address this problem by being highly specific about the components of the portfolio. My daughter's sixth-grade teacher used this approach. For example, draft writing components *must* include a 1-page outline (100–120 words), two drafts, and a final draft. Furthermore, many teachers simply note the presence or absence of certain items, not paying attention to their quality. This simplifies the procedure and renders grading more uniform and less subjective, but it also has the effect of shifting the portfolio back toward traditional assessment in its inflexibility and reliance on quantity and not quality. Each of these decisions carries complex and usually contradictory moral consequences.

At this stage in the book I hope it is not necessary to point out that the preceding discussion is not intended to argue against portfolios. As I mentioned, I continue to use portfolios myself, and I see them as being considerably superior to traditional forms of testing. My point in this section is that even if we choose to use portfolios or other forms of alternative assessment, we still very much need to be aware of the moral consequences of our decision and the moral complexities with which it is fraught. It is only through reflection on these issues that we can move toward what for us is a morally grounded approach to evaluation.

CONCLUSION: IS MORALLY JUSTIFIABLE ASSESSMENT POSSIBLE?

The preceding discussion suggests another central moral paradox of language teaching. On the one hand, without some form of evaluation our students cannot be sure of their progress or how this matches up with the requirements of the systems within which they are studying; furthermore, although administrative convenience may seem a paltry motivation for particular forms of testing, it is also true that it represents one domain in which learners are treated in some way equally. (One could also argue that, in principle, an efficiently functioning administration should also be in the best interests of students.) On the other hand, *any* form of testing or assessment that we use is unavoidably only a partial, indirect, and subjectively judged reflection of the student's actual abilities; this is true both because of the inherent qualities of assessment procedures and the impossibility of ever conclusively determining what it means to know a language. Thus, we have a moral imperative to offer some form of assessment, yet any form of assessment is morally suspect and fallible.

This clearly leaves us as teachers in an uncomfortable position. Is there any way out of it? Well, at one level there is not; like the other moral paradoxes and dilemmas we have examined in this book, the paradox of testing simply represents a constant factor in our work. It is better seen as a dynamic rather than a problem; that is, it is simply a permanent characteristic of what we do, rather than some obstacle that will eventually be overcome.

On another level, however, I believe there are ways forward. First of all, I suggest it is incumbent on each of us as teachers to continually reflect on our own values and continue to question whether these values are accurately reflected in our assessment procedures. A few years ago, when I was in graduate school, I took a course in transformational syntax from William O'Grady, a well-known theoretical linguist. Assessment for the course was based on three extremely tough sit-down examinations as well as a term paper. At the very beginning of the course, O'Grady explicitly justified his use of examinations by saying that we were future teachers of linguistics and so we needed to know the material in detail. I happen to disagree with this argument, and under other circumstances I might have polemicized with O'Grady; but I was very favorably impressed with the fact that the professor had questioned his own assessment procedures and had made decisions about how to evaluate the students not out of an unthinking adherence to custom but out of a conviction (I would further suggest, a moral conviction) that it was the good and right thing to do, and furthermore, that he respected his students as thinking adults enough to explain his position to them.

This brings me to another key component of our role as teachers in determining assessment procedures. All educational work is fundamentally rooted in context. In the case of assessment, then, I suggest that we have an ongoing moral duty to interrogate the context in which assessment is being used, in order to determine what is the good and right way to proceed with these particular learners at this particular point in their learning. In the case of Professor O'Grady, a key element in the equation were the needs of the students in their coming professional lives: His learners were all doctoral students in linguistics, and so the examination format was, in his view, appropriate. In any given case, this equation will be a complex one, including the future needs of students, their expectations, the nature of what is being assessed (vocabulary? writing skills? communicative ability?), systemic requirements, cultural preferences, and so on. Moreover, calling the decision-making process an *equation* is also inaccurate, because in reality the weighing of many factors is nearly always done in a holistic and flexible way.

It is equally important to interrogate the nature and ostensible and real purpose of existing tests: that is, to take what Shohamy (1998), after Pennycook (1994) and others, called a "critical" approach to language testing. According to Shohamy, among other things such a stance:

- "views language tests as ... deeply embedded in cultural, educational, and political arenas where different ideological and social forms struggle for dominance" (p. 332);
- "asks questions about what sort of agendas are delivered through tests and whose agendas they are" (p. 332);
- "challenges psychometric traditions and considers interpretive ones" (p. 332);

- "asks questions about whose knowledge the tests are based on," including whether what is included in tests can be "negotiated, challenged and appropriated" (p. 333);
- suggests that "the notion of 'just a test' is an impossibility because it is impossible to separate language testing from the many contexts in which it operates" (p. 333).

The one key word that Shohamy (1998) did not use, although she implies it in all the foregoing, is *value*. What values are enshrined in, or presupposed by, the kinds of tests we use and the ways in which we use them? Whose values are these? What kinds of value, in turn, are assigned to students on the basis of these tests? I suggest that in addressing the moral complexities of teaching each individual teacher needs to consider the values inherent in the tests used in her own educational setting.

Finally, though I am rendering myself particularly vulnerable to attack here, I would strongly advocate the need for flexibility in assessment procedures. Given the multiple uncertainties that attend the design and the taking of a test, we simply cannot rely on raw, unmediated scores to give us accurate and fair information about a student's level, ability, or amount of learning. The learning process is a highly individual one, and the teacher–student relation is similarly unrepeatable. If assessment is to be an integral part of teaching—which, I have argued, it needs to be—then it must be included in that relation, inside what Noddings called "the uniqueness of human encounters" (1984, p. 3). This does not exclude the use of externally written and scored standardized tests, but I believe that, in essence, assessment in the classroom must be brought within the bounds of the unique relation between teacher and student and that in order for this to happen, we need the flexibility that comes from a deep knowledge of our students and their circumstances. Of course, it is also clear that another word for this flexibility is *subjectivity*, and to misquote a famous saying as it might apply to teaching, the price of subjectivity is eternal vigilance.

QUESTIONS FOR REFLECTION AND DISCUSSION

1. Look again at the situation described by Wen-Hsing. How would you have handled this situation? What other options were open to Wen-Hsing? What values would underlie these options?
2. What did you think about the story of Alison's student in French? Would it be reasonable to apportion blame in this story? How else might it have been resolved?

3. What forms of evaluation do you use in your own teaching? What values underlie these kinds of evaluation?

4. What do you think we should be assessing in the testing of language learning? How can tests or other forms of assessments measure this? What problems are there?

5. To what extent should we as teachers be responsible not just for students' learning but also their study habits, their behavior, and their values?

6. What, in your view, is a good student?

7. Liz Hamp-Lyons (1998) suggested that test preparation programs are ethically (morally) wrong. What is your view of this? Have you prepared students of your own for standardized tests such as the TOEFL? In light of your experiences, what do think of Hamp-Lyons' arguments?

8. Have you had any experience with alternative forms of assessment? If so, what problems of values did they give rise to? From a moral standpoint, do you agree with my position that alternative assessment is preferable to traditional kinds of assessment?

5

Three Facets of Language Teacher Identity

Teacher identity is a complex and difficult concept. It is complex because the question of "who we are" evokes a vast array of both complementary and contradictory responses. It is difficult because, of all the matters considered in this book, it is the closest to the core of what it is to be a person and a moral agent and thus to the most sensitive issues of all.

The word *identity* is often used as if it were something relatively permanent, unitary, and uncontroversial. Yet recent thinking on identity has challenged such assumptions (Gergen, 1991; Norton Peirce, 1995; Norton, 1997; Sarup, 1996; Schrag, 1997). Rather, identity is seen, among other things, as fundamentally relational in nature, and thus as negotiated through language and other forms of social interaction; as contested and the site of conflict; and as being in constant flux and change. I argue here that these qualities are reflected in different aspects of the identity of English teachers.

The topic of teacher identity in English language teaching (ELT) is only now beginning to be explored (Duff & Uchida, 1997; B. Johnston, 1999a; Varghese, 2001b). It is clear even from this emergent literature that teacher identities are complex things indeed; the matter deserves separate treatment elsewhere. In this chapter, I do not attempt an exhaustive account of language teacher identity; rather, I want to look in detail at three aspects of teacher identity that seem to me to be particularly rich in the dynamics of values that are the object of my interest in this book. These aspects are as follows: First, I look at the teacher's identity in the teacher–student relation, including the moral rights and responsibilities of the teacher in this relation. Next, I take a close look at the matter of professionalism, in particular the extent to which the identity of "professional" forms part of language teacher identity. Third, I consider the place of religious beliefs in ELT, specifically as they relate to the teacher's sense of spiritual identity.

THE TEACHER–STUDENT RELATION

The conflicting moral values underlying the stories I have been telling in this book are common across many contexts and incidents; but these values are always mediated and negotiated by the relation between a particular teacher and a particular learner or group of learners at a particular point in time and in a particular context. Recall, for example, the case of Young in Mary's class, discussed in chapter 2. In that situation, Mary's decisions—first to give Young lots of time to respond, then to stop insisting—arose from her own personality; from her understanding of Young's personality; and from her knowledge of the class as a whole, which she had gained from working with the same group of students daily over the previous weeks.

The teacher–student relation is the foundation of moral interaction in language teaching. It has certainly been central in our understandings of the situations described and analyzed in previous chapters. Also, given that identity is fundamentally relational, as pointed out earlier, a crucial part of teacher identity is bound up with the teacher–student relation. In this section I look at two aspects of the teacher–student relation and its unique incarnation in each classroom and context: teachers' involvement in their students' lives, and the balance between authority and solidarity in teacher–student relations.

Involvement in Students' Lives

In his wonderful book entitled *To Teach: The Journey of a Teacher*, William Ayers (1993) recounted an incident that occurred right at the beginning of his career as a teacher, in an elementary school. A child came to school without lunch money, and Ayers lent him the 50 cents he needed to buy lunch. Ayers tells how the collective wisdom in the staffroom strongly discouraged these kinds of interaction, on the basis that if you did this once, you would "be buying every kid lunch every day" (p. 14). Ayers disregarded this advice, concluding laconically of his colleagues' prediction: "It never happened" (p. 14).

I mention this story because, among many other things, it reminds me of how as teachers we are constantly coming into contact with our students' lives beyond the simple learning and teaching of subject matter. I want to say right away that I do not believe, and do not argue here, that teachers *should* be deeply engaged in the lives of their learners beyond the subject matter of the classroom. My argument is that *some* level of involvement is inevitable, and that this adds a further complex moral dimension to our relations with students and thus to our identities as teachers.

I have known many teachers who do in fact become extensively involved in the lives of their students: teachers who frequently invite students to their homes, take students to the dentist, or socialize with them in the evenings and on weekends. I have also known many good teachers who do not see their students at all socially, believing that their responsibilities toward, and contacts with, students end with the close of the school day. In considering all the different cases and kinds of relationships between teachers and learners I have seen over the years, it seems clear to me that the nature and level of this relationship has to be determined by each teacher and in each context; there is no fixed right and wrong. Yet it is also clear that, however the relationship evolves, determining and negotiating it is a moral matter that needs to be given serious thought by each teacher.

Whatever position we take, though, it is inevitable that we will encounter situations in which the personal lives of students enter into our educational relations with them. This seems to me a logical extension of the nature of teaching. First, as repeated examples in preceding chapters have shown, all teaching involves acting on the world; in some way, we are always in the business of changing our students. Furthermore, there is never a clear dividing line between the student as student and the student as person. Indeed, much contemporary methodology has strongly emphasized the "whole-personhood" of each learner (Stevick, 1990). Thus, try as we might, we can never satisfactorily segregate our influence as teachers from our influence as people; and, even more crucially, we can never fully separate our relations as teacher and student from other aspects of relations between people—put another way, we can never satisfactorily separate the educational content of the teacher–student relation from its other components.

Let me share a couple of examples of what I mean, taken from my own experience. A few years ago, one of my students, a Christian Arab woman, came to my office and, in the middle of a discussion about her term paper, burst into tears and began to tell me about her problems with her fiancé, who was getting cold feet about their marriage and putting off their wedding day. (Before I go on, let me add at once that eventually the situation was resolved, and the couple are now happily married.) Another female student fell behind in her work because she had a miscarriage during the course she took with me. A third, a doctoral student who was teaching Spanish, came to me for advice because her own department was concerned about negative comments about her personality (specifically, her "moodiness") that had appeared on student evaluations.

What all of these situations have in common is that, whatever my response to them, I had to have *some* response: These were not things I could ignore. And in thinking about how to handle the different situations (a process for which I had precious little time in some situations, for example, with a student in tears in my office), the same kinds of moral considerations present themselves. I had to juggle my role as fellow human with my role as teacher. With the student who was falling behind, for example, I could not merely sympathize; I had to deal in some way with the fact that she was absent from class and not doing the work but that she was very anxious to be able to complete the class. This, in turn, leads to a dilemma rooted in the justice-versus-caring debate: I had to deal with each case individually, while remaining certain that other students in different yet perhaps comparable circumstances would receive the same consideration.

It is also important to observe that although as teachers we can control the extent to which we ourselves encourage particular kinds of relations—we can decide, for example, whether or not to invite students to our house for dinner—there are also many cases where matters are out of our hands, because of things that happen to the students (such as the miscarriage) or because of things that our students choose to tell us—that is, the students' own agency (like the student who came to me with the problem of her teaching evaluations). A male EFL teacher in Izmir in western Turkey once told me about a young female student of his from the more traditional eastern part of the country whose father had forbidden her to see her boyfriend; she was so miserable that she felt suicidal. What was the teacher to do with this information? Not to say anything is as much a moral act as getting involved in some way. Furthermore, in the great majority of cases our training as teachers does not prepare us for such situations; they come upon us in our professional roles, but we have little more than our human instincts and our own life experiences to guide us.

Getting involved in our students' lives, then, is not a clear-cut choice to which we can unproblematically say "yes" or "no." We already *are* involved in their lives, by virtue of being their teachers. Furthermore, relations are two-sided; this means that we cannot always be in control of what directions they take. Thus, our identity as teachers must constantly be renegotiated within the changing contexts of relations with different students, and we ourselves must continually re-evaluate our own beliefs and expectations and those of our students regarding what the boundaries of our involvement should be.

Authority and Solidarity

An important moral aspect of the student-teacher relation that is crucially linked to teacher identity involves the delicate balance that we strive to maintain between what might be called *solidarity* and *authority*. On the one hand, we want there to be solidarity between our students and ourselves. We want to be on the same side as our students—for our interests to be their interests, and for them to be aware of this and to see us as allies. On the other hand, we want to retain the kind of authority that will allow students to respect us and treat us seriously, both for reasons of relation and also so that the business of teaching and learning may proceed effectively. Every individual teacher aims for a unique balance between these two opposing wishes, and the position of any teacher may shift as her career develops. Yet I believe that all teachers wrestle with the same two opposing notions in negotiating their identity in relation to their students.

A very thoughtful and detailed account of this tension is given in a paper by Ana Maria Barcelos (2001), a young teacher in a university language center in Brazil. Barcelos outlined the general *dilemma*—using just that word—as follows:

> On the one hand, teachers have to keep distance from students and to maintain discipline in order "to demonstrate to those outside the classroom that students respect them" (Feiman-Nemser & Floden, 1986, p. 508). On the other hand, teachers are required to "form personal bonds with students in order to motivate them to learn" (Feiman-Nemser & Floden, p. 508). Feiman-Nemser and Floden (1986) remarked that this tension creates an ambiguity in teachers' role and remains a central issue for beginning as well as experienced teachers. (p. 81)

Barcelos described her own situation thus:

> I was the youngest teacher at the university where I taught and I looked a lot younger than I actually was. More than once, students mistook me for a student. My age and my young appearance, and the fact that I had once been a student at that university made me feel insecure about my authority as a teacher. This aspect is probably common to many new teachers in their work places. Nevertheless, I felt it was especially true for myself, first, because of the age

> difference between the other teachers and I, as I already mentioned,
> and second, because I was the only teacher who did not have a Mas-
> ter's yet. These two aspects probably made me more self-conscious
> of my authority as a teacher in class and perhaps more susceptible
> to students' comments and criticisms. (p. 85)

Barcelos's (2001) article is a follow-up analysis of data from a
study she conducted that looked at the beliefs and expectations of her own
students and at how these beliefs and expectations related to her own as the
teacher. The problem Barcelos found as she investigated her students' beliefs and expectations was that many of them felt that it was her responsibility to exercise more authority and display less solidarity (what Barcelos
called bonding or closeness) in the class. In some cases, they made more
general comments to explain how they preferred strict teachers. For instance, one student said: "Sometimes the teacher asks students to write an
essay for homework. The student won't do it if the teacher doesn't control it,
if the teacher thinks we will do it. We don't have time. Now if teacher forces
us we find a way and time to do it anyway. If the teacher demands, we will
find a way" (p. 87). Other comments were more overtly directed at Barcelos
herself, accusing her of being "too nice." For instance, she reported:

> On the last day of class, when I asked them to evaluate the course
> orally, a student said that I should have been stricter and more de-
> manding and should have imposed more discipline. Another student
> commented: "You can't be like that with students (do whatever they
> want) because they will take advantage of the situation." (p. 88)

Possibly the most interesting part of what is throughout a very engaging article is Barcelos' (2001) analysis of her own response to the findings of her study. She reported considerable feelings of guilt and
inadequacy as she reflected on what she heard from her students. Yet she
wrote that, although her students' comments seemed to suggest that she
should change certain aspects of her teaching, she resisted making such
changes because they ran counter to her own values and beliefs—that is, to
the teacher identity that she wished to claim for herself. It is in this more
than anything else that her dilemma is moral in nature:

> Should I follow my students' beliefs about the role of the teacher as
> a controller or follow my philosophy of teaching in which the role
> of the teacher is that of a facilitator? I could not find a place in the
> middle where I could stand. I saw myself between two forces: my
> culture of teaching and my students' culture of learning, i.e., their
> beliefs about language learning. [...] I was trying to establish a
> close relationship with students and an affective positive language

learning environment. However, my students expected me to play a different role and exercise more control. If I chose to continue *to be who I was* [italics added], students might have perceived me as an incompetent teacher. However, neither did I want to adopt a role that was not part of my philosophy. Either option would bring me a problem. (pp. 89–90)

For Barcelos, the tension between authority and solidarity is a moral one that involves the core of her identity ("to be who I was"). Note that this core is itself relational, because what Barcelos means, I believe, is to be who she is—that is, to take on an identity she feels to be true to herself—*in relation to her students*. The tension is also complicated by a further dilemma: To what extent should we listen to our learners? This is also a dilemma of the teacher–student relation. We want to be on the same side as the learners, yet their expectations of the relation are often different from ours. We are committed to listening to our learners, yet sometimes we hear them saying things which we regard quite simply as wrong. To what extent should we follow their expressed desires, and to what extent should we use our authority to impose practices that we feel entirely confidently to be in the learners' best interests? This conundrum underlies many aspects of teaching; for example, we often hear students complaining about communicative teaching methods and saying that they want more grammar teaching. How are we to respond morally to these requests?

It is also worth quoting Barcelos' (2001) conclusions in her article. Her story is not resolved; the tension between authority and solidarity remains. She wrote:

By portraying my dilemma I hope other teachers have been able to recognize themselves in this report and that it has helped them not to feel inadequate or odd in their constant struggle to adjust. As for me, it has helped me become more knowledgeable about my own identity as a teacher and to accept myself as imperfect, as "a teacher in progress"—in progress in my language proficiency, in my philosophy of teaching, and in my practice. Dilemmas can bring a lot of frustration, but they can also help us to become stronger if we learn how to consider our students' beliefs not as erroneous but as starting points for analysis of our own teaching. (p. 94)

Barcelos's (2001) work reveals several of the aspects of teacher identity I outlined earlier. As already mentioned, it shows the way in which identity is fundamentally relational in character; as a consequence, it is also something that must constantly be negotiated socially. Also, identity is not fixed or permanent but is constantly changing. Barcelos's notion of a "teacher in progress," echoing Kristeva's (1984) wider view of the "subject-in-progress," captures this aspect of teacher identity perfectly. Underlying all these qualities of teacher identity, as I hope I have shown, are profound moral dynamics that go to the heart of our own understandings of ourselves both as teachers and as people.

VALUES AND PROFESSIONALISM

The idea of professionalism is one of the most contested concepts in ELT. Studies, articles, and opinion pieces continue to address the question of whether or not ELT is a profession and whether teachers of English as a second language (ESL) and English as a foreign language (EFL) are professionals (e.g., Edstam, 2001; B. Johnston, 1997; Maley, 1992; Nunan, 1999a, 1999b; Pennington, 1992). These writings typically revolve around the same set of issues, and usually ask whether ELT bears the traits of established professions: control over its own practices; control over membership of the profession; an orientation of service; high status, social recognition, and rewards; and so on.

In my view, this discussion is partly unproductive and partly useful. It is unproductive because to a large extent it is setting us as teachers against established professions such as medicine and the law, and I think that it is unrealistic to imagine that in most societies teachers of English (or indeed of any subject) could acquire the same status and rank as doctors and lawyers. Furthermore, as Welker (1992) pointed out, teaching is a different kind of occupation than law and medicine, insofar as, unlike doctors and lawyers, as teachers we hand over the knowledge and skills we have to our learners. More generally, as I hope I have made clear in this book, the teacher–student relation lies at the heart of education, whereas one could argue that the lawyer–client relation, for instance, is less moral and more instrumental in character. Last, as Popkewitz (1994) and others have pointed out, there are dangers involved in the professionalization of teachers that are often overlooked in calls for professionalism. These include systemic requirements for greater accountability, which in some cases have led to unacceptable increases both in teacher workload and in the monitoring of teachers' practices, and the questionable association of professionalism with "objective" scientific knowledge and political neutrality.

On the other hand, the discussion of professionalism in ELT is useful because it draws our attention to an ongoing contradiction in our identity as teachers and in the values underlying our work. I would like to explore this contradiction through quotations from two teachers about professionalism. The first quotation comes from an interview with Bea, an experienced American EFL teacher currently teaching English at a private university in Japan:

Interviewer: Do you see yourself as a professional and, if so, how do you understand that term?

Bea: Yeah, militantly so. [*laughs*] Never used to be, but after going through the wars of being adjunct composition faculty—that, you know, the sort of lowest on the ladder, never tenured, never secure […] And now working abroad, um, I don't even entertain any notions of tenure in Japan. I mean, it's just a concept that there's so much resistance to and so few foreigners have ever been given tenure in university systems. Um, and there're so many ways for them not to give you tenure that it would be really stupid to think, "oh, but, I'm going to be different. I'm going to be the one that … " No. Not even thinking it. This is purely adjunct for me. But, because of all that, it also makes me much more aware of having to really work to continue to see myself and do things to see myself as a professional, in order to kind of, I hope gently, force other people to see me as a professional, because, institutionally, it's not there. Um, I think if you're, you know, given the title, given the tenure, given the office, you know, whatever the trappings are, the retirement plan [*laughs*], the golden retirement plan, you know, it may be easier to just sort of assume you're a professional, and you don't have to think about it. But the systems I've worked in have always marginalized folks—me and folks that have done my job. So, I mean, if *I* don't do things to see myself as a professional, nobody else is going to. And it really *is* important, self-esteem-wise, or else you feel used, you know, and that's gonna translate in the classroom. (B. Johnston, Mahan-Taylor, & Pawan, 2001)

In this part of the interview Bea raises a number of the major issues associated with the contested nature of professionalism and identity as a professional in ELT. She talks about the marginalized position of many teachers and programs, a matter I examine in more detail in chapter 6, and she explicitly draws the connection between this aspect of teacher identity—professionalism—and teachers' work with students ("that's gonna translate in the classroom"); that is, the teacher–student relation. What most interests me, though, is what I see as a conflict of values implied in what Bea says about her own identity. Bea says that she "militantly" considers herself a professional and talks of the need "to really work to continue to see myself and do things to see myself as a professional." Yet at the same time she acknowledges that other people in the context in which she works, and specifically those in the university administration, do not share this view: that "institutionally, it's not there." This seems to me to pinpoint a fundamental tension in ELT professionalism: that although many teachers strive to be professionals, their aspirations are not reflected in the way their work is perceived by those around them. In other words, there is a disjuncture between what can be called *claimed identity* and *assigned identity*. (Ana Maria Barcelos's [2001] dilemma of authority and solidarity, discussed earlier, can be seen as another clash of claimed versus assigned identity.)

However assigned identity is seen by actual individuals, the important thing is that it is encoded, formally or informally, in the sociocultural and political structures of the context—for example, the unavailability of tenure for non-Japanese teachers that Bea discusses. This is a classic case of the importance of contextual features in understanding values.

At first glance, it might seem as if this contradiction is more of a difference between Bea's own personal, internal views and the views of others around her. However, I would argue that in fact the conflict is an internal one—in other words, that the opposition I have described here also exists within the teacher and is thus a dilemma of the kind that we have been analyzing elsewhere in the book. I think it is not unreasonable to suggest that Bea is not an island and that the views of others also exist inside her, in Bakhtinian fashion (Bakhtin, 1981). Certainly she presents her own view of herself as a professional not as a natural and effortless thing but as a struggle, saying that she has to "really work" to maintain this view; the implication is that part of this work involves convincing *herself* that she really is a professional, so that others will also be convinced. Yet this struggle is not easy. It seems rather clear that the clash of values represented by the two views of teacher identity is also an internal moral dilemma. Once again, as well as being morally charged, teacher identity is also contested and (aggressively here) negotiated, both internally and externally.

Bea's guiding principle in this struggle seems to be " if *I* don't do things to see myself as a professional, nobody else is going to." This attitude enforces her identity as agent, as someone who does not have to accept assigned identities, but can act on the world to claim a different identity. However, such an attitude can be hard to maintain, and is not always possible in the different contexts of ELT. This is shown by the next extract, from an interview with a young Polish teacher called Joanna whom I spoke with a few years ago as she was beginning her teaching career. Joanna had been identified by her university supervisor as a particularly able and promising teacher, but she had the following to say when I asked her if she was a professional:

> I think I could be; but I'm not, at school, because I don't have time to organize my classes in such a way that they would look like, as if, well, they are organized by a professional person; because I'm not working as much as I could perhaps to get the most of the book, and the time I have; well, and all other possibilities. But I'm not going to do more because first of all I don't have time, and secondly it's not paid enough to work more, I think; and then I'm not going to do something, as I said I'm not an altruist, and it's a cheat-off, actually, what we're doing, with the, well, the Ministry of Education, and what's going on in this country, I mean the work you have and the money you get for it, I think it's a huge misunderstanding and I'm not going to put up with it. (Johnston, 1997, p. 705)

Joanna's impassioned statement—half confession, half defiance—reflects the same clash of values Bea described, but Joanna comes to a different conclusion. She too acknowledges that, like Bea, she has a vision of professionalism for her own identity as a teacher (this is implicit in the admission that "I'm not working as much as I could"), and she also shows the lack of recognition of her work from the broad educational context ("it's a cheat-off, actually, what we're doing, with the ... Ministry of Education, and what's going on in this country, I mean the work you have and the money you get for it"). Yet in Joanna's case she chooses *not* to claim an identity as professional, but rather to protest the identity she is assigned by the system in a different way: by consciously refusing to act like a professional. I have interviewed many teachers about professionalism, and the overwhelming majority have told me that in principle they see themselves as professionals, or at least would like to, whereas the systems in which they work often do not reflect this image. I always remember Joanna's words, because she is one of the few teachers who have admitted that they do not at present aspire to professionalism. Also, I am struck by the fact that, like Bea's, Joanna's response to this dilemma is also a moral one in that she too is seeking to resolve the inherent contradiction between internal expectations of professionalism and the external failure to support these expectations. Joanna, however, rather than trying to influence the external failure, decides simply to re-evaluate the expectations themselves.

In Bea and Joanna, then, we see two different possible responses to the moral dilemma of professionalism and identity as a professional in ELT. It is not my place to adjudicate which is "right" and which is "wrong." I do think, though, that professionalism in ELT will in most contexts continue to be an uphill struggle, and while I admire Bea's resolve, I also understand (and perhaps even also respect) Joanna's refusal to be taken for granted. I have often heard teachers accusing themselves and others of excessive volunteerism in their work, and it is true that many teachers I know put in many more hours than they are paid for and do not complain. However, the accusation of volunteerism—seen here as being in opposition to professionalism—also reveals another aspect of the moral dilemma underlying professionalism. Teachers who "go the extra mile" do so often out of a sense of duty; that is, out of a moral belief they hold. It is this value that clashes with the value of self-respect and the respect of others that Bea and Joanna touch on. Striving to be a professional in ELT inevitably involves negotiating this conflict of values too.

RELIGIOUS BELIEFS AND ELT

The third facet of teacher identity I wish to examine is also one of the hardest to write about: the place of religious beliefs and beliefs about religious practices in what it means to be a teacher.

I acknowledge right away that this section will be predominantly speculative in nature. To the best of my knowledge there is no literature specifically addressing the subject of the religious beliefs of language teachers and how their beliefs and values influence their actions as teachers. Thus, what follows is based on one or two anecdotes and on my own reflections. Even more than many of the subjects raised in this book, the issue suggests an important focus for future research.

Language Teaching and Religion

Though there is no literature directly concerning teachers' religious beliefs and values, there is a fair amount of work documenting the intimate relation between language teaching and organized religion at the sociopolitical and cultural level.

First, throughout the colonial period the major Christian denominations aggressively engaged in missionary work that supplemented the political, economic, and cultural colonization processes pursued by the European powers (see chap. 3). As Phillipson (1992) expressed it: "Promotion of religion, language, and national economic and political interests have often gone hand in hand" (p. 32). The "natural" superiority of the Christian religion dovetailed with the "natural" superiority of the English language and the European way of life that, as Phillipson explicated in detail, provided the philosophical underpinnings of colonialism. In many cases the Church was a major player in the global spread of English. Phillipson cited a Church Missionary Society report on primary education in Sierra Leone, dated 1808: "The great object which the parents of the children had in sending them to school was their acquirement of the English language. Therefore, according to their strict instruction, not a word of Susu was allowed to be spoken in the school" (Tiffen, 1968, p. 71, cited in Phillipson, 1992, p. 187).

Phillipson (1992) also pointed out (p. 126) that in many Church schools instruction was conducted in local languages. This fact, however, does not mean that the Church or the other colonizing forces supported indigenous language instruction; rather, they found this the most efficient way both to proselytize and to pursue the other goals of colonialism.

This latter aspect of the work of missionaries must also be borne in mind. Wosh (1994) described how in the 19th century the American Bible Society became a significant commercial undertaking, with a major part of its income deriving from missionary work abroad, for example in the Levant (the eastern Mediterranean) (pp. 151–174). Stoll (1982), on the other hand, analyzed the more recent work of the Summer Institute of Linguistics, also known as the Wycliffe Bible Translators, in preparing Bible materials in the indigenous languages of Latin America. Stoll revealed how in the 1970s this organization was "an official arm" (p. 2) of the governments of South and Central America and how its powerful influence collided "spectacularly with Indian civil rights organizing and Latin American nationalism" (p. 2). Furthermore, at a spiritual level, Stoll wrote that "translators continued to use the languages of native people to campaign against their religious traditions" (p. 2). Thus, even where the Church's role involves the use of local languages rather than colonial languages, it is evident that it continues to play a part both in the promotion of Christian religious beliefs and in the sociopolitical, economic, and cultural hegemonies of the colonial and postcolonial worlds.

Language Teachers and Religious Beliefs

What really interests me, though, is something else. As I have repeatedly stated, I am interested above all in language teachers themselves. When it comes to religious beliefs, I am particularly fascinated by the ways in which teachers' beliefs affect what they do in class and in their schools. It seems to me that of all the different kinds of beliefs we can hold, religious beliefs are often the most personal, the most deeply held, and the most closely linked with our identity. In thinking about values in language teaching, for many individuals when one comes to religious beliefs one has reached foundation.

Of course, for exactly the same reason this subject is extremely difficult to write about. Beliefs about religion are among the most profoundly significant parts of identity, and so they should be of great interest to anyone wanting to gain a proper understanding of identity in teaching and classrooms, yet at the same time they are not rooted in the kind of logic and reasoning that the academy trades in. It may be this fact that discourages researchers from investigating religious beliefs and values in education. In this section, I try to open up a discussion on this topic, but I recognize that it will not be easy.

Although I am not usually a fan of the confessional style of writing, I think that in this particular case it is important for me to explain my own religious beliefs, so that you can know the perspective that I bring to what I have to say. I am an atheist; after struggling for many years with Christian beliefs, quite recently I finally concluded that I could not believe in a supreme being. For many years before that, I had grown increasingly averse to organized religion of any kind, seeing it as usually political rather than merely spiritual in nature. At the same time, I recognize that there is a profoundly spiritual dimension to human life (I hope what I have said in this book about moral values supports this claim), and furthermore that this spiritual dimension has a strong social element: It is almost always the case that people of any given religion gather together for the purposes of prayer, religious rites, and so on. In fact, the vast majority of the world's population practices some kind of established religion, and I would be foolish not to understand that my own position is a distinctly minority view. However, it is a sincerely felt one, and of course it cannot help influencing the discussion of religious beliefs that follows here.

I should also add that, despite my own views, religion is a major presence in my life. My wife and children are practicing Catholics. Several of my coworkers are Jewish, and students and others with whom I am in frequent contact come from a broad range of religious backgrounds, including Islam; Buddhism; Hinduism; Native American spirituality; and, of course, the gamut of Christian denominations. I believe profoundly in respect for the spiritual beliefs of others.

This last statement leads me to one of the most important issues I have encountered. Having myself wrestled so long to gain a proper understanding of my own religious beliefs, something that puzzles me is how individuals can, along with their beliefs about their own spirituality, also believe that they have a moral duty to convince others that this religion is right for them too; that is, their beliefs include the certainty that their religion must be spread.

Let me give a small but telling example. A student of mine worked in a nonprofit school in the Twin Cities in Minnesota that offered among other things, ESL classes for adults. The school was supported partially by federal grants. Another ESL teacher at this center began each day's classes with a reading from the Bible. He did so despite the fact that, because the center was supported by government money, it was illegal to include any kind of religious practices in the instruction that the center offered. His belief in the importance of performing this reading outweighed the risks involved.

What fascinates me about this case is not the teacher's religious beliefs themselves but the fact that he felt an obligation to enact them publicly with his students. I want to set aside for a moment the question of what his students felt about his practices and concentrate on the motivations of the teacher concerned. It seems to me that this example reveals in miniature many of the myriad complexities of religious beliefs in teaching.

The first reaction of many teachers to this situation is to condemn the teacher concerned, or at least his actions. I confess that this was also my own initial response. Yet I find myself also trying to understand why a teacher would act in this way. Though I was not able to talk to the teacher himself, I find the anecdote to be a very rich source of reflection. It seems to me that his actions must have been motivated by a sincere and profound belief that he *had* to read the Bible to his students—that this was a moral duty. The duty must have been all the more keenly sensed given that the teacher was prepared to break the law to follow it. In this light, I have to conclude that it is very hard to argue that there is something *inherently* wrong with this teacher's actions. I have repeatedly made the point in this book that our work as teachers fundamentally and essentially involves acting on the world, and that what we have to decide is exactly what form that action should take. For most of us this involves selection of materials, ways of interacting with students, and so on. Yet, as I have said, our decisions in these matters are always moral in nature. The teacher I just described has also made a morally-based decision, one grounded in his deepest beliefs; he has come to the conclusion that his own form of moral action should involve openly sharing his religious faith with his students.

The story outlined earlier, then, reveals at least two important moral dilemmas regarding the place of one's religious faith in one's teaching. From the teacher's perspective, there is the question of the extent to which one has the right or the responsibility to extend one's religious practices so that they include others, for whatever reason (from the story as it was passed on to me by my student, it was not clear whether the teacher concerned was attempting to proselytize or merely sharing his religious practices in a social setting).

From the point of view of others who disagree with this teacher's practices, it seems to me that there is a significant dilemma in responding to them and to him. As I have tried to suggest, I believe that it is extremely difficult to find truly convincing arguments against these practices. As teachers, we are involved in changing students for the better; this teacher's way of going about it is different from that of many others, but his goals seem to be the same. Ultimately, our rejection of his practices can only be based either in legal arguments (which are only indirectly related to moral judgments) or in our own beliefs, themselves rooted in faith , like the teacher's, not in logical argument.

Of course, I hope it is clear that the reason I have included this story and have spent so much time discussing it is not because the story itself is so shocking or unusual but because it is indicative of a significant current in ELT: that of missionary work and more generally the links between ELT and the activities of various churches, both in English-speaking countries and especially abroad. Many of my own students have worked as missionaries or are planning to work for religious organizations in non-English-speaking countries. The moral concerns and dilemmas I have outlined here also underlie their work. This has been a much-ignored issue in ELT research and in the professional discourse of the field. There have been occasional, rather incidental mentions of this topic (for example Julian Edge's [1996b] article and the subsequent exchange of letters in *TESOL Matters* that it provoked), but a sustained dialogue has failed to emerge. More promisingly, at a recent TESOL convention MaryAnn Christison convened a panel in which several prominent figures in ELT described the ways in which their religious beliefs influenced their work as teachers and teacher educators. This kind of self-exploration offers a valuable start in the process of uncovering and analyzing the relationship between religious beliefs and the work of teachers and institutions in ELT. However, a lot of thinking, research, and writing still needs to be done. I hope this section of the present chapter will stimulate more interest in the topic and encourage researchers, and especially practicing teachers and others involved in ELT, to take an honest and thoughtful look at the role of teachers' religious beliefs in the practice of ELT.

Dealing with the Religious Beliefs of Students

Finally, I look at another important aspect of religious beliefs in the classroom: the response of teachers to the religious beliefs and practices of the students.

In all teaching, there is a potential for difference between the religious beliefs of the teacher and those of the learners. In ELT, though, such clashes are endemic to the nature of the occupation. Whether we are talking about ESL classes in Britain, America, Canada, or Australia, expatriates teaching abroad, or in many cases EFL teachers teaching in their own country where that country is itself multicultural, in ELT there is a very high probability that the teacher's religious beliefs do not coincide with those of all the students, and furthermore that the students themselves come from a diversity of religious backgrounds.

One of the most striking and difficult cultural encounters for teachers and students to manage is that between the English-speaking cultures of Britain and North America and that of traditional Islamic cultures. Many Muslim students are profoundly shocked when they come to the United States to study. I heard one story recently of a student who was so shaken by what he saw at the airport on his arrival that he left to go back home the next day and never joined the program for which he had come.

In some Islamic countries, educational authorities are often anxious to avoid the clash of cultural values to be found in Western coursebooks while simultaneously embracing the English language. A Lebanese Muslim woman teacher who taught in United Arab Emirates for some years before studying with me put it roughly like this: In such contexts, teachers and students want only the language, without the cultural baggage that goes with it. She justified this further by pointing out that many students need English primarily for occupational purposes (e.g., in fields such as chemistry or engineering) and have no need of additional cultural information.

Yet there is no clear dividing line between culture and language. Indeed, many in the field of language teaching believe that all language is thoroughly and irrevocably soaked in culture, and that it is an impossibility to learn the language without the culture. Certainly, a student in the United Arab Emirates may be able largely to avoid cultural phenomena if he is only reading an engineering textbook, but the moment he needs to come into contact with American or British colleagues, cultural norms of inter-action will enter into the language being used.

One frequent cause of friction between Arab students and Ameri-can teachers in our own Intensive English Program at Indiana University is the question of gender roles. Many male Arab students are shocked to be taught by female teachers and feel uncomfortable being in a class with fe-male students, especially if those women are from other cultures and dress in ways that are considered unacceptable in strict Islamic settings. Female teachers, in turn, complain that many students do not take them seriously or treat them with respect.

Such conflicts, I suggest, are an integral part of language teaching; they are not problems to be overcome once and for all but are part of the permanent moral landscape of our occupation. Also, to a significant ex-tent, the question of how teachers deal with each instance of clashes is a moral matter of identity. To what extent is the teacher prepared to change in order to accommodate the religious values of the students? To what ex-tent does she feel it morally imperative to take a stand, at the risk of offend-ing or alienating her students? How is her own religious and cultural identity related to her professional identity as a teacher?

Finally, the problem of certainty raised in the previous section returns here from a different perspective. The third paradox raised by Edge (1996a) is: "How do I exclude the right to aggressive totalitarianism from the right to be different?" (p. 21). Edge (1996a) took as his starting point the 1992 murder of Hitoshi Igarashi, the Japanese translator of Salman Rushdie's novel *The Sa-tanic Verses*; Igarashi's slaying was related to the fatwa imposed on Rushdie himself. Edge (1996a) emphasized that this is not a question of Islamic faith: "The problem is not in Islam; the problem is in certainty: the kind of certainty and the attitude associated with it that some people feel gives them the right to impose their views on others—if necessary, to the point of death" (p. 21). (This formulation of the matter calls to mind the murders here in the United States of doctors who perform abortions, killings that the perpetrators have justified on Christian religious grounds.)

Murder, of course, is an extreme act. But Edge's (1996a) broader point applies to all of us: Given that, for many of us at least, part of our professional morality entails respect for other beliefs and other values, what do we do when faced with students whose values do not include such respect for the values of others? Can we be tolerant of intolerance? This is one of the hardest moral dilemmas faced by language teachers, and it goes to the heart of who we are as teachers: for, as Edge (1996a) pointed out, it brings us up against what he calls "cultural bedrock" (p. 24), in other words, the most profound values from our own religious and cultural foundations.

The reason I have dwelled on the topic of religious values at such length is that it is one of profound personal importance to me. I am fascinated by the powerful dynamic between doubts about what one believes and feels and the moral duty to try to convince others of one's beliefs; between the urge to do the right thing and the need for, and yet dangers of, some kind of certainty; and between the need for tolerance and the quest for foundation. The one thing I know for certain is that without the opportunity to bring such matters to consciousness and to reflect on them intellectually, the crucial role of religious beliefs in ELT will never be properly understood.

CONCLUSIONS

The three facets of teacher identity discussed here are in many ways disparate and may appear unconnected. Nevertheless, I believe there are powerful common underlying themes that link aspects of identity as diverse as teacher–student relations, professionalism, and religious values. As should be clear from the preceding analyses, in all three aspects teacher identity can be seen as relational—primarily, of course, in relation to students, but also to one's colleagues, one's background and national affiliation, and so on; as being in permanent flux, both for internal reasons of growth and the constantly changing external context (that is, in Barcelos's [2001]words we are always "teachers in progress"); and as existing in dynamic conflict, often between claimed identities and assigned identities.

Beyond this, though, all three facets reveal the links between the identities of teachers in the sphere of the language classroom and the broader identities that they bring in from the outside world. In each case, teacher identity cannot be understood by looking at the classroom alone. In the case of teacher–student relations, the identities created by and for teachers in their relations with students are rooted in their identities as people as much as in their professional identities as teachers. As far as professionalism is concerned, a primary conflict is between inner values of professionalism and the perceptions of the outside world. Last, religious values clearly come from outside the classroom, yet the beliefs and values of both teachers and students affect classroom interaction in important ways, and religious identities that might go unchallenged outside the classroom can find themselves in confrontation within it. In all these aspects, the dynamics of teacher identity are saturated in moral meaning and dilemmas of values; this adds yet another dimension to the complex moral topography of ELT.

QUESTIONS FOR REFLECTION AND DISCUSSION

1. I mentioned the fact that different teachers get involved with the lives of their students to differing degrees. Which of the following might you do?: take a student to the doctor or dentist, help a student with immigration forms, invite students to dinner at your home, go to a restaurant or bar with your students, go to a movie or concert with your students, take a vacation with your students.
   How do you decide which of these things you would do and which you would not do? What criteria do you use to determine what forms of interaction and involvement are acceptable or desirable and which are not? Has this changed over your career as a teacher?

2. I briefly mentioned three personal problems that students brought to me. What problems have your students brought to you? What was your response? In hindsight, how else might you have handled these situations? What moral values were at play in them? What did you learn from these meetings?

3. Consider Ana Maria Barcelos' (2001) story about the dilemma of authority and solidarity. What did you think about her stance? What is your position on this dynamic? Have your views changed over time? Is it possible to generalize about this dilemma in language teaching?

4. Another aspect of teacher–student relations that is often discussed is that of respect for the teacher. For example, some American teachers do not allow students to wear caps in class or to chew gum during the lesson, on the grounds that this shows a lack of respect for the teacher. What is your view of such rules? What kinds of rules do you have in your own classroom? How do you justify these rules pedagogically or morally? What happens when they are broken?

5. Do you consider yourself to be a professional? What does this mean to you? How are you perceived by your students, your colleagues, your superiors, and those outside of teaching? What do you personally do to enhance your image as a professional, either in your own eyes or those of others? What values underlie your attitudes to professionalism? Specifically, how do you feel about what is said by Bea and by Joanna in this chapter?

6. How do your religious beliefs affect your teaching? To what extent does a teacher have a right or a responsibility to share her religious beliefs and values with her students?

7. Have you ever encountered intolerance in your students? How did you handle it? What values play a part in determining how to respond to students who express intolerant views in your classes?

6

Values in Teacher Development

INTRODUCTION: TEACHER DEVELOPMENT
AS A MORAL PROCESS

In this chapter I look at the processes of teacher development and suggest the values, and clashes of values, that underlie them. As elsewhere in this book, I argue that this aspect of our work as teachers is profoundly rooted in values and moral judgments.

I need to begin by explaining what I mean by *teacher development*. The term is used in rather different ways in the two professional contexts in which I have worked the longest: Europe and North America. In North America, teacher development is usually seen as something done by teacher educators and teacher trainers for (one might say, to) working teachers. It usually takes the form of in-service workshops, courses, summer institutes, and the like.

By contrast, in Europe, in English language teaching (ELT) at least, teacher development is something that teachers themselves undertake and that is guided by the teachers concerned. It is this understanding of teacher development that I use in this chapter. The other kind of teacher development is fine—indeed, I conduct a lot of in-service workshops and so on myself—but I think it is very important to start from a view of this process which places the teachers in control. In this understanding, your development is something you yourself initiate and pursue; other people—me, for example—can help and guide you, but others cannot tell you what you need or what you should do. It is a very deeply held value of mine that teachers must always be seen to be in charge of their own development.

This said, what exactly is meant by *development*? What do *I* mean by it? This is another important point that needs to be clarified before I go on. I see teacher development as a broad set of processes all revolving

120

around the professional and personal growth of the teacher concerned. Teacher development is *not* merely a matter of "improving one's teaching" or "becoming a better teacher." These things obviously play an important part in what it means to grow as a teacher, but I believe that they cannot in themselves constitute a sufficient value to drive teacher development. Teacher development is a form of teacher learning and I am in full agreement with Edge (2001c) and with K. E. Johnson and Freeman (2001) that we cannot expect students to go on learning in class if their teachers are not also able to go on learning. I acknowledge that this attitude rests in belief as much as in fact: Research has not (yet) given us direct evidence of a link between student learning and teacher learning (although efforts are being made; see Johnson & Freeman, 2001). Nevertheless, all my years of experience as both a teacher and a teacher educator have shown me that this link is one of the most powerful driving forces behind effective education, and that no school, program, or educational institution can function effectively without taking into consideration the development needs of its teachers.

I further argue that the drive toward teacher development is fundamentally grounded in values. A moment ago I took pains to dissociate teacher development from a narrow understanding of improving one's teaching. Yet I made my point only to make some room for teachers to select their own focuses for their development. Given this freedom, many teachers do indeed choose to direct their efforts toward enhancing their classroom practice, for example, addressing what they see as weak points in their teaching or introducing new ways of doing old things. The fact that teacher development so often takes this form reflects an underlying value: that of doing a good job and making sure that students learn. Thus, the value of effective education directly drives a great deal of teacher development.

Yet this is not the only value inherent in teacher development. Many teachers seek not to change what happens in their classroom but, at least initially, simply to understand it (Allwright, 2001). The drive to understanding, in turn, also constitutes an important value. Indeed, it is one of the most profound values in education: one of the attitudes teachers most desire to instill or encourage in their students is an innate interest in, and curiosity about, various aspects of the world around them, whether it is the structure of the human body, the history of one's country, or, in our case, the language we are trying to teach. It seems to me that the desire to understand part of one's own corner of the world—one's own classroom—both reflects and models the desire to understand that we most want our students to have. Furthermore, as I show later, in many cases the desire to understand revolves around core moral features of the classroom such as the student–teacher relation.

Last, I argue that the commitment to growth and to personal and professional development is itself a value. I follow Taylor (1992) in believing that concern for one's own fulfillment—what Foucault (1988) called "care of the self"—is not a narcissistic or selfish enterprise but reflects a profoundly held belief in the value of individuals (as also reflected in the humanistic psychology of Maslow [1959] and others). In teachers this value is especially important, for two reasons: First, because it is tempered with the concern for others that occupies the much greater part of teachers' time and energy, and second, because it is the same value that we espouse as teachers with regard to our students. Indeed, it seems to me that we would be guilty of hypocrisy by claiming that each student needs to be treated as an individual and to be encouraged to grow and yet simultaneously claiming (or merely assuming) that teachers themselves do not need these kinds of opportunities. If we are to see our students as individuals, then we must apply the same yardstick to ourselves as their teachers.

The notion of teacher development as a moral process is not new. Sockett (1993), for example, described teacher professionalism as being not merely an "instrumental" matter but having a "moral core" (p. 13), because "the moral good of every learner is of fundamental importance in every teaching situation" (p. 13). Even closer to the spirit of this chapter is the work of Jack Whitehead (1993), a British teacher educator and proponent of action research. For Whitehead, teacher development is driven above all by a perceived tension—what he calls a "paradox" or a "living contradiction"—between a teacher's educational beliefs and her practice. Characteristically phrasing this in the first person—for the teacher's own perception of this tension is the most important thing in the processes of teacher development—Whitehead expressed it as follows: "I experience problems when my educational values are negated in my practice" (p. 69). The notion of values is clearly the central point of this dilemma. Taking another perspective on the same dilemma, Whitehead asked: "How do I live my values more fully in my practice?" (p. 17). In both these formulations the centrality of values, and the dynamic nature of the paradox or (as I would put it) the dilemma underlying teacher development, show that Whitehead's view of teacher growth is very close in spirit to my own.

These, then, are the attitudes and beliefs underlying what I have to say about values in relation to teacher development. In this chapter I begin by looking at values inherent in the ways teachers have found to take a close look at their own classrooms and their own work, using such frameworks as action research, exploratory practice, cooperative development, and narrative inquiry. Next, I consider the broader teaching life and the question of career development in ELT. Then I look at the matter of advocacy in the field of ELT, returning to the political dimensions of our work from chapter 3. Last, I say a few words about values in relation to formal teacher education programs.

VALUES AND TEACHER RESEARCH

Over the last 10 or 15 years, it has become increasingly common for teachers to conduct investigations of their own classrooms and to present their investigations at conferences and in publications. A commonly used framework for investigations of this kind is *action research* (Burns, 1999; Edge, 2001a; Edge & Richards, 1993; Freeman, 1998; Nunan, 1989; Wallace, 1998); although other frameworks have also been employed, including *exploratory practice* (Allwright & Lenzuen, 1997; K. A. Johnson, in press), *cooperative development* (Boshell, in press; Edge, 1992, 2002 [see especially chap. 11]), and *narrative inquiry* (K. E. Johnson & Golombek, in press). I subsume all of these different ways of paying sustained attention to one's own classroom, and of making the results of this attention public, under the heading of *teacher research* (TR), a term I am borrowing in a somewhat cavalier fashion from Freeman (1998), among others. I also apologize in advance for not explaining in detail how these approaches function; rather, I refer you to the sources I have just cited for more practical information of this kind.

I see work in TR as being grounded in values, in at least two significant ways. First, the very act of investigating one's own classroom reflects particular values. Second, TR offers a particularly appropriate framework for examining the moral dimensions of one's own classroom.

The Underlying Values of TR

The whole TR movement, and its incarnation in ELT, emerged as a reaction to existing power relations in educational research in which "experts" (university researchers) produce knowledge for the consumption of "practitioners" (teachers). At a practical level, it was recognized that the kinds of knowledge which emerge from what I call *traditional* research bear only an indirect relationship to the kinds of knowledge that teachers need, and that the ways in which the knowledge is presented often make it hard for teachers to use. Beyond this, however, there is a broader question of the image of the teacher implicit in such a relationship: The teacher becomes a consumer of knowledge and a technician applying the findings of research. In this relationship the teacher's own role is not valued. The various kinds of TR, on the other hand, place significant value in the teacher herself and in her interests, her understandings, and her capacity for gathering information and making sense of it. In other words, it recognizes—it *values*—the teacher's role as an active participant in the production of knowledge and understanding.

One concept often used to distinguish between traditional research and TR is that of the ownership of knowledge. This refers to the fact that in traditional conceptions of research and of knowledge about teaching, the knowledge is "owned" by external experts, whereas in TR the knowledge is "owned" by the teachers and learners who both produce and use it. Although I wholeheartedly approve the idea underlying this notion, I feel that the image of ownership tends to emphasize an economic—that is, an instrumental—view of TR stressing above all the question of resources. What is more important, I believe, is the fact that TR represents a higher value placed on the teacher and her contribution. In TR, the teacher's involvement is valued. Her own quest for knowledge and understanding is seen as being at least as important as that of external researchers, and her skill in gathering and analyzing data is also acknowledged. In all these things, the teacher is, quite simply, taken seriously. I believe that it is this fact above all that shows how the promotion and practice of TR is rooted in a particular set of values about teaching and learning; that is, it is moral in nature.

Other moral aspects of TR follow from this basic orientation. First, a great deal of TR is collaborative in orientation, involving cooperation both with one's colleagues and one's students. I see this as representing a more general belief in the value of collegiality and dialogue.

As far as colleagues are concerned, it has long been recognized that teaching is an "egg-box profession" (Freeman, 1998) in which teachers are carefully kept separate from each other and the act of teaching—and, consequently, of planning teaching beforehand and reflecting on it afterwards—is traditionally carried on alone. Collaboration with colleagues, on the other hand, is not simply a different way of doing things but constitutes a fundamentally different underlying belief, one that stresses the importance of cooperation, dialogue, and the working through of shared understandings and processes of seeking understanding. This belief is not restricted to collaborative action research (Burns, 1999) but is reflected, for example, in any school or program that encourages teachers to observe each other's classes or to cooperate on curriculum development or materials design. I would argue that an orientation to the social nature of teacher learning is one of the single most important values that should underlie teacher development.

A corollary of collaboration with colleagues is collaboration with learners. Traditional educational research sees learners primarily as subjects: things to be studied. TR, on the other hand, emphasizes the importance of involving learners in the processes of the research (Branscombe, Goswami, & Schwartz, 1992). Many TR studies include the active participation of the learners in posing and seeking answers to questions (for an excellent example of a study that used an action research framework, see Auerbach & Paxton, 1996). As noted earlier, this element of the research process is not merely a new technique but indicates a profound underlying difference of values. The active involvement of learners in the research shows that their knowledge and understandings too are valued; it also valorizes the teacher–student relation, which, as I have repeatedly argued, is the foundation of the educational enterprise.

Also, TR not only acknowledges, but actively requires, the autonomy of the teacher or teachers concerned. It is an approach that is predicated on a teacher's ability to make independent judgments and decisions about aspects of her classroom practices. As such, TR is grounded in beliefs about the need for teachers to operate under conditions of relative autonomy and is thus opposed to a view of teachers as merely technicians enacting practices and using materials provided by others from outside the classroom. This too is a moral perspective on what is important in teaching.

Last, TR represents the fundamentally change-oriented nature of teaching. Not all TR projects are or should be aimed at change (Allwright, 2001), but TR is grounded in the basic truth about teaching, mentioned several times in this book, that all teaching is about changing other people. Two further consequences stem from this. TR places the *agency* of the teacher center stage, acknowledging its importance, and it follows the assumption, also mentioned here before, that any change must be assumed to be for the better—that is, that it is morally justifiable. By placing change at the center of the research process, rather than at the end as occurs in traditional educational research, TR also recognizes the centrality of moral values in the educational process.

In all these things, TR embodies a particular set of values concerning the nature of teaching and being a teacher. It thus constitutes not merely an alternative set of practices in educational research, but also an alternative set of values regarding what, and who, is important in finding out about teaching and learning. I suggest that the inclusion of both teachers and learners finally humanizes all aspects of educational research: that it recognizes the humanity, and thus the agency and autonomy, of those who participate in education, instead of regarding them as objects to be manipulated by others from outside. It is above all in this humanization of research on teaching and learning that I see the fundamentally moral nature of TR.

Looking for the Moral in One's Own Classroom

The second way in which TR carries moral significance is that it is an ideal vehicle for teachers to explore the moral dimensions of interaction in their own classrooms. Although TR projects can and do focus on a broad range of issues of teaching and learning, TR, much more than traditional educational research, is well suited for the difficult job of looking at the complexities of moral interaction in the classroom. Such complexities are often much more apparent to the people involved than to "experts" from outside. In addition, because of the value it places on the teacher–student relation and on action and agency, TR is better placed than traditional research to capture the morally meaningful events and incidents of the classroom. In this section I look at two studies that investigated moral aspects of classroom interaction. The first used action research techniques to look at dialogue in a graduate classroom; the second employed narrative inquiry to describe a elective on volunteerism in a U. S. intensive English program.

A few years ago, when I began teaching graduate classes, I conducted an action research project in which I examined dialogue in my methods class (B. Johnston, 2000). I chose this topic because, while it seemed to me that dialogue was, generally speaking, something to be desired and encouraged in class, I did not know exactly what I meant by that, or what manifestations of dialogue there actually were in my class. Thus, my project was aimed not at some problem I wanted to fix but at the desire to better understand my own classroom.

I have chosen to write about this study here because, aside from its moral significance as an example of TR (as explained earlier), it also focuses on issues of values in its subject matter. Through the study I was seeking to understand the nature of dialogue in my class. Dialogue, in turn, as I have already pointed out, is a crucial component of the teacher–student relation (Noddings, 1984).

My initial notion of dialogue was associated above all with classroom discussions. However, as I analyzed the data I had gathered, I came to understand that dialogue took place not just in in-class interaction but through a multiplicity of channels, including dialogue journals, process writing, negotiations of syllabus, and even informal encounters in hallways and in my office. This range of different possibilities proved important, for example, for quieter students. One or these, Qiu, a female student from Taiwan who had been largely silent during class discussions, nevertheless carried on a lengthy exchange with me in her weekly dialogue journal. In her final journal, in which she was asked to reflect on the journal itself, she had this to say:

> For me, writing in English doubles the burden because I have to think about the form in addition to the content. But I really like to keep a journal like the way we did as a channel of mutual communication. You emphasized that it will not be graded; so I feel released to the grammatical errors in my writing. Besides, something I can not respond immediately and directly in class, I still can express later in journal and, as you can find that I always reflect what we have discussed in class to my own experience and to the situation in Taiwan. [...] Your feedback is always encouraging and inspiring. Your suggestion reminds me of things which I have not thought about and provides me another angle to look at a matter. (B. Johnston, 2000, p. 166)

Qiu's comments helped me to understand that dialogue can, and sometimes must, take place outside the physical classroom. Two other aspects of dialogue are raised in Qiu's journal excerpt. First, Qiu affirms the importance of paying attention to what the student has to say and not (as is our constant tendency as language teachers) to focus on *how* it is said. Second, through data such as these I was forced to acknowledge the crucial part that my own voice played in the dialogue. As the teacher, I also had an obligation to say my own mind and to share my experience; not to do so would be to fail to play my part in the dialogue and thus in the teacher–student relation.

These were some of the findings of my study. Others included the fact that dialogue does not simply mean "saying things"; that is, each student making a contribution to the discussion. Rather, dialogue involves give and take; it requires participants not just to listen to each other but to respond by building on or challenging each other's contributions. Last, I came to understand that dialogue is crucially sensitive to context and inescapably emergent: That is, it is not something that can be "introduced" once and for all into a class, but needs to be continually encouraged, nurtured, and monitored.

In all these things, my TR project both reflected my own values as a teacher and teacher educator and helped me to see the complexity of moral relations in my own classroom. The matter of shy students, for example—a constant feature of work with non-native speakers, especially those from certain cultural backgrounds—has always been of concern to me; through this study I acquired hard evidence of the value of "alternative" channels of dialogue with such students. More generally, through data such as student evaluations I found confirmation for my belief in the value of a dialogical approach.

The second example of TR is set within the framework of narrative inquiry (K. E. Johnson & Golombek, in press). Suzanne House (in press) used this framework to recount her experience teaching an elective course in volunteerism in the Intensive English Program of Ohio State University. The title of her article—"Who Is in This Classroom With Me?"—hints at the fact that, like my article on dialogue (B. Johnston, 2000), it too takes a close look not just at relatively technical aspects of classroom practice but at the teacher–student relation, and at the attitudes and above all the values that different students bring to class.

House (in press) acknowledged that when she first began work on designing a course on volunteerism, "I was thinking mainly of the pedagogical and linguistic knowledge I would need to make the class a success." Yet as the course got under way, she came to understand that "[t]he most important knowledge I needed for this class was information about the perspectives and values of the students." In other words, she became most interested in the student side of the student–teacher relation. The course that House designed involved a mixture of classroom-based discussions and actual participation in volunteer activities: Students "explored the issues of poverty, hunger, homelessness, and aging" and also "sorted food and clothing at a local pantry, painted sheds for Habitat for Humanity, and chatted with residents of a retirement community."

Through the experience of reflecting on the course and writing about it, House was able to explicitly state the values that underlay her own decision to create the class: These included "my belief in volunteering as a humanitarian activity" and "my desire for students to see beyond their own often privileged experiences." Both of these motivations are primarily moral in nature. The first constitutes one of House's fundamental beliefs about what it means to be a good person; the second is a clear indication of the teacher's role in changing students in a way that she judges to be for the best.

What is equally interesting, though, are the students' responses to the class. One of House's discoveries about the students was, in a few of them, an "eagerness to regularly disparage American society and American people." House confessed that she "backed off" on addressing comments of this kind "because I wasn't feeling equipped to deal with harsh condemnation from students whose language skills—or cultural discourse styles—kept them from any semblance of tact." This, of course, is a moral decision and one which involves the teacher's role as de facto representative of her own national culture (see chap. 2).

Even more interesting were the attitudes of some students to volunteering itself and to the social problems it addresses. House reported that some of the Japanese participants "strongly believed that with education and effort, very few people would actually need the services we explored"; whereas "students from poorer countries" were "much more inclined to accept the idea that the people we met were not entirely responsible for their difficulties and situations." One activity that House designed involved the students devising family budgets for a couple with two children in a situation in which the husband had been laid off from a well-paid job for which he was trained, and now both parents were working in low-paying jobs. House recounted that "some of the Japanese students spent the class period insisting that this couple should never have had children they could not afford [...] They were unable to grasp the idea of a competent worker being laid off [...] In their eyes, the only explanation for being poor was personal failure." The same students, House reported, regarded the homeless as people who had "made the choice not to work." House ascribed these beliefs to cultural background, but I would add that there must also be an element of individual beliefs, too: first because it was only some of the students who raised these objections, and second because I have heard Americans (and others) voicing the same attitudes toward the poor and the needy. In any case, differing beliefs about social phenomena such as poverty and the need for volunteerism revealed a profound clash of values concerning the goals and content of the course.

It is interesting that House also revealed clashes of values regarding the form of the class. Half of the class of 12 students constituted a group of Japanese teachers of English. House reported that these participants "chose to critique my teaching methods during class time." There was also what House herself called a "clash" of expectations regarding her role as teacher: While she saw herself as "a teacher and fellow volunteer who could offer some cultural and linguistic knowledge and was prepared to use pedagogical knowledge to provide a learning experience for the students," the students expected her "to be a cultural expert with explanations for the actions of all American citizens as well as the American government." This conflict of basic beliefs about what teaching is supposed to involve is no less dramatic or central for its being terribly familiar to many teachers who have tried to implement communicative or other alternative approaches to teaching in cross-cultural contexts.

From the point of view of this chapter, though, the most significant thing about this experience was what House herself learned from it and the fact that she chose to crystallize her learning in the form of a public document. House wrote that she:

> gained and made use of knowledge about my students as learners and as people. As a teacher, I am constantly drawing on an extensive range of ways of knowing that I have acquired, and it is tempting to believe that this makes me more unique than anyone else in my classroom. If I could simply impart hard-earned wisdom to similar students who all want and need the same information, teaching would be an easy art. I know, however, that the complexity of what I bring into the classroom is matched by the complexity of what students bring to the same room. Not only do the students possess a multitude of experiences, beliefs, and goals, but each student will—must—make decisions and choices that may or may not have anything to do with the influence of the teacher or the class.

This passage accurately conveys the moral complexity of teaching, in which the values and actions of the teacher must interact with the values and actions of the learners, with unpredictable results. It is this understanding of the moral dimensions of her classroom that House was able to acquire through TR (in this case, narrative inquiry). Here, as with my own dialogue study, it is through reflection and writing that the complex moral realities of the class can be properly acknowledged and examined.

VALUES AND CAREER DEVELOPMENT

At the opposite end of the spectrum from TR projects focused on individual classes lies the broadest matter of the careers in ELT. In this section, I say a few words about teachers' careers and specifically about the moral dimensions underlying the way these careers develop.

Of course, many people, myself included, have questioned whether such a thing as a career in ELT even exists. Empirical studies that have been conducted (e.g., Centre for British Teachers, 1989; B. Johnston, 1997; McKnight, 1992) have suggested that in many contexts, a teaching "career" is a rather messy thing: In the absence of formalized "career ladders" teachers are left to their own devices to determine what for them constitutes forward or upward motion, with the result that there is a huge amount of variation in the ways in which teacher's professional lives unfold, including a lot of what might look like sideways movement (and a sizeable dropout rate).

Yet as time goes on, more and more people are pursuing master's degrees in ELT-related subjects (teaching English to speakers of other languages (TESOL), teaching English as a foreign language (TEFL), applied linguistics, etc.), and I find myself meeting older teachers (say, in their 40s and 50s) more frequently. It would seem that many people are indeed staying in ELT. It seems valid, then, to talk about career development in ELT, even if for many of us our careers do not have the same linearity and obvious structure and coherence as careers within well-established occupations.

I also want to emphasize that for me the notion of career development is an important one. We are teachers, and our prime responsibility is to the people we teach. Yet our own lives are also important and, as I have said already, my concern is with teachers themselves. I believe firmly that teachers have not just a right but a responsibility to care for themselves and their professional lives and that this right and responsibility are an inalienable part of what it means to be a teacher. Thus, to those who would object that speaking of teachers' careers is not a matter that belongs in applied linguistics, I would say that it must belong, for, as was the case with teachers investigating their own classrooms, without proper care of teachers we cannot have proper care of learners—this is both a philosophical and a practical impossibility.

What do I mean by *career development*? I mean the things we choose to do with our working lives, seen from the broadest perspective. This may mean: changing jobs; taking on a different kind of teaching, for example, one that involves a new skill area or elective topic, or learners of different ages or ability levels to those with whom one has previously worked; getting involved with curriculum design and renewal; taking a promotion; returning to school to study for a master's degree or a PhD; moving into a position of responsibility, such as section coordinator or department chair; moving into administration, for instance, as director of studies or principal; deciding to write teaching materials for publication; and many other possibilities.

As we move through our professional lives, at certain points we seek out opportunities such as those just listed; in other cases, the opportunities come looking for us. Whether the initial impetus is internal or external, though, all through the process of such potential changes we are faced with a series of decisions. Should I apply for promotion? Should I accept the job I've been offered? Should I reduce my teaching load to make time to write a book? Am I happy focusing on teaching, or would I like to take on administrative duties? Should I apply for the new position in the language center across town? Should I stay here or emigrate? Should I stay in English teaching or look for better paid work?

All of these questions are of great importance in the lives of teachers. Some of them, as can be seen, are particularly momentous, involving one's whole life (and the lives of one's family). Yet it is also the case that in the ELT literature little if any sustained attention has been paid to teachers' lives at this level.

I suggest that decisions of the kind exemplified earlier that teachers face are, like the other kinds of decisions examined in this book, moral in nature; that is, they revolve around values held by the teachers concerned and around dilemmas in which teachers have to weigh competing values.

In such cases, of course, the values involved are not only narrowly professional. Eleven years ago, my wife and I made the momentous decision to move from Poland to the United States so I could enter a doctoral program. It goes without saying that I very much wanted to pursue doctoral studies, so from my individual point of view the move was desirable, especially because I was accepted into a good program in Hawai'i. But the decision to come to the United States, initially for 4 years, was far from straightforward for the rest of my family. My wife would suddenly find herself halfway round the world from her family, with whom she has always been very close, and would also be plunged into a second-language culture with which she was unfamiliar and in which neither of us had any relatives on whom we could rely for help. Furthermore, we had three young children at the time. Was this the right move for them? We spent long, long hours weighing the advantages and disadvantages of the move: that is to say, considering the opposing values involved. To this day I am not entirely convinced that it *was* the best thing for all three of the children; although they gained a great deal of linguistic and cultural experience, they were also deprived of the closeness of family in Poland and England that all five of us hold as a crucial value.

I tell this story because I think many readers will find that parts of it resonate with their own experience. The nature of the ELT profession is such that a great many career moves simultaneously involve geographical displacement, and the already complex decisions that such potential moves involve are very often further complicated by the needs and wishes of one's family. Family finances are an important consideration, offsetting the often considerable costs of obtaining qualifications against the hope of higher earning power later. All of these concerns must be juggled with the teacher's own desire for further education—the drive to professional development that underlies most of what I have been discussing in this chapter.

It is important, of course, that that drive itself be rendered explicit. A couple of years ago a former master's student of mine named Chris called me to ask if I would write him a letter of recommendation for his application to a doctoral program. As we talked about his plans, I asked him why he wanted to obtain a doctorate. He was brought up short; he thought for a moment, and then said: "You know, throughout this whole application process [he had already talked at length with the professors in the program to which he was applying], no one's asked me that question." We broke off our conversation so Chris could think about his motives and goals. He called again a few days later and was able to articulate his reasons to his own satisfaction; he is now well embarked on his program. But I was struck by the fact that his motivation had never come up in his discussion with his future professors. I feel that this is an occupational hazard of working in university settings: We, the professors, automatically and unthinkingly assume that pursuing a doctorate is the best career move. For many teachers it is not. Another master's student of mine was about to enter a PhD program but decided instead to open her own language school offering tuition in the business sector, and found the work to be just the kind of challenge she wanted at that time. The important point is that for the crucial dimension of values underpinning our career decisions to be made apparent, we need to be able to articulate our motives and the beliefs that underlie them.

Of course, the ultimate career move is to leave ELT altogether. When I was interviewing EFL teachers in Poland in November 1994, a time of rapid change and great uncertainty in Polish society, many of the Polish teachers spoke about the possibility of leaving teaching. Rafał, who was in his mid-20s, was teaching English in a prestigious high school; he was also studying in business school. He told me openly that he was looking to find work outside of teaching.

Interviewer: So you're going to drop out of teaching?

Rafał: I think so, because generally speaking the English language teaching market, the language teaching market, is predominantly female, because it's something women can afford to do who have let's say husbands who make good money and who don't have to support themselves from what they earn. And personally I don't see any chance of leading any kind of normal life if I'm supposed to be a good teacher who devotes most of his time to teaching. It just isn't physically possible. (B. Johnston, 1997, pp. 698–699; interview originally conducted in Polish)

What can be said about Rafał's comments? From the perspective of values, I suppose it is hard to question the personal desire to advance in life. In Rafał's words (here and elsewhere), though, I am struck by the lack of a discourse of professional fulfillment to counterbalance the materialism apparent in his goals. His remark about how ELT is "predominantly female" is technically correct, although of course it begs the vital sociopolitical question of why this means that it is poorly paid. I am also concerned for his students: What often happened in these times in Poland was that there was a very rapid turnover of teachers in any given school, and so students often ended up repeating the beginning level of English several years in succession, in the absence of any continuity. Of course, teachers cannot develop their careers purely on the basis of their learners' needs; yet the discourse of service seemed signally absent in my interviews with Rafał and with other teachers. It was a particular lack in the professional discourse of ELT in Poland at that time. Without it, I feel that the moral substrate of teaching as a whole was also impoverished, to the detriment of all concerned in Polish education, but especially the students and the teachers.

MARGINALITY AND ADVOCACY IN ELT

In the literature looking at teachers' professional lives and careers, a powerful recurrent theme is that of marginality and marginalization (see, e.g., Edstam, 2001; B. Johnston, 1997, 1999a; Pennington, 1992), a subject already mentioned by Bea in the interview excerpt in chapter 5. This aspect of our work as teachers is so pervasive that it needs to be discussed here as a separate issue in relation to teacher development.

One of the reasons that the notion of marginality is so prevalent in language teaching is that it covers a wide range of related phenomena. Marginalization affects professional and academic relations; it is also social and political; and it concerns psychological questions of identity.

First of all, marginality is political in the broader sense of the status—that is, value—ascribed to those who teach ESL and EFL and the resources available to them. It is this marginality that Joanna, the Polish teacher, referred to in the passage quoted in chapter 5 when she talks of the "cheat-off" associated with the Polish Ministry of Education. ESL and EFL teachers in a large number of countries are underpaid and overworked, they lack job security or benefits, and they generally suffer from a lack of recognition from authorities such as governments and ministries of education. In this regard, to a significant extent English language teachers suffer the same fate as teachers in general: the de-skilling (Popkewitz, 1994) and semiprofessionism (MacLure,

1993) that have increasingly beset the work of teaching also affect our work in ESL and EFL. Of course, teaching has never been a strong and autonomous profession such as medicine or the law (see chap. 5). Part of the reason is that teaching is done mostly by women, and the lower status accorded women in most societies is reflected in the status accorded to teachers in those societies. Partly for the same reasons, teachers are often marginalized from decisions regarding their work; the decisions rather are left to those who do not have direct contact with schools and classrooms, such as local, regional, and national educational authorities, university specialists, school boards and so on.

Yet there is also a specific marginality associated with ELT even in relation to other aspects of the educational enterprise. This intraprofessional marginality is clearly exemplified in the United States. Here, ESL teaching is at the very bottom of the pecking order in most schools, and ESL teachers along with it. In many schools, ESL classrooms are even physically marginal, located across the playground in prefabricated huts rather than in the main building of the school. In others, ESL teachers are considered a luxury and are the first to be reassigned to cover classes when a "regular" teacher is absent. Often there is a shortage of teachers, which means that teachers are overworked; many serve more than one school. Other schools, of course, have no ESL teachers at all, regardless of how much they are needed. In many schools, because of a lack of qualified ESL specialists other teachers, unqualified in ESL, are assigned to teach ESL classes. Everywhere there is a lack of funds and resources. Of course, I am not suggesting that the situation in all other countries is the same, or even that all ESL contexts in the United States match this description. Nevertheless, I have seen and heard enough, from teachers in many states and many countries, to know that elements of such stories have echoes in many other contexts.

Mention of "ESL specialists" in the preceding paragraph leads me to the third and final aspect of marginality; the kind that exists at the level of personal identity. An overwhelmingly popular sentiment regarding language teaching is that "if you can speak the language, you can teach it." This underlies what Phillipson (1992) has labeled the "native speaker fallacy" (pp. 193–199) and leads to the entirely unjustified valuing of native speaker over non-native speaker teachers the world over. (A Japanese student of mine once told me about a language school in Tokyo that employed only teachers who were not only native speakers of American English but they also had to be blond.) However, this attitude, which is one of the most pernicious misconceptions in the entire field of language teaching, also leads to what I see as other distortions of values.

Above all, the equating of speaking the language with being able to teach it leads to marginalization in the sense that a teacher's knowledge—including the complexities of pedagogical knowledge, pedagogical content knowledge (Shulman, 1987), and teacher–student relations—is reduced to knowledge of language. For native speakers, this translates into a lack of appreciation for the conscious knowledge of language that other native speakers do not have and that is acquired only through training and work in the field of ELT. A colleague and I once conducted a study of grammar teachers' knowledge of English grammar as used in ESL classes (B. Johnston & Goettsch, 2000). We asked one native speaker teacher where she gained her extensive knowledge of the English grammatical system; she said: "Doesn't everybody know this?" (p. 449). The answer, of course, is that no, they don't. I would argue that this teacher enforced her own marginalization in failing to appreciate the value of her own professional knowledge. It is interesting that the same lack of appreciation was to be found in many of the Polish teachers with whom I spoke. These teachers embraced the identity of "expert speaker of English" while simultaneously downplaying their pedagogical skills (Johnston, 1997). This too reinforces marginality, by systematically devaluing the level of skill and knowledge required to do the job well; it is another variant on the adage cited earlier.

Finally, I wish to briefly mention another aspect of social and professional marginalization. The expatriate teachers in Poland whom I interviewed (B. Johnston, 1999a) often felt sidelined in Polish society. Even as, at one level, they were "lionized" (in the words of one of them) by their students, at the same time they were excluded from certain aspects of both their professional work (for example, decision-making) and their personal lives. The same phenomenon is mentioned by Bea in the interview quoted in chapter 5, in which she talks of the difficulty that native speaker teachers have both in assimilating to Japanese society and in playing a significant role in the workplace—and this in a context in which they are financially comfortable and in otherwise rather high-status jobs in universities. This aspect of marginality also recurs across numerous national and regional contexts.

Of course, there are certain advantages to marginality. I have experienced this many times in my professional life. When I was teaching in Poland, the English language center where I worked was part of the university, but it existed outside the structure of schools (colleges) and departments. Thus, we were free to design our own classes and organize things in whatever way we saw fit. We were not subject to the controls and expectations of a regular academic department. When I was in graduate school, on the other hand, as an advanced PhD student I taught undergraduate classes in the

Teaching English as a Second Language program. The faculty of the department didn't really want anything to do with these classes, because they were busy with their own graduate classes and their research, so I had very little in the way of supervision, and could pretty much design the syllabi and run the classes as I saw fit. In both these examples, being on the margins allowed me relatively free rein to provide the best teaching I could without unwelcome attention from above; I was "off the radar screen." American teachers have told me that the marginal status of ESL in schools in the United States has often empowered them into various forms of quiet but effective resistance that are possible only when the administration doesn't think of you very often, is ignorant of what you do each day, or does not have the time or the inclination to check up on you frequently.

Marginality, then, can in some circumstances lead to empowerment and an opportunity for subtle forms of resistance (Giroux, 1988). However, I would argue that at the same time it leads to a lack of resources and a lack of appreciation for what teachers do; in other words, to a failure to *value* teachers in ELT. This brings me to my second topic of this section: the matter of advocacy.

I believe that all our talk of teacher professional development is seriously compromised if we ignore the marginalization of ELT that is staring us in the face, that is, if we treat the professional growth of teachers as something that can be both conceived and carried out without reference to the sociopolitical realities of teachers' lives. To devalue this central feature of work for huge numbers of teachers is to fail to grasp the significance of the drive for professional development. I believe that ELT professional organizations have unwittingly colluded in this artificial separation of the professional and the political. For many years, for example, the TESOL (Teachers of English to Speakers of Other Languages) Convention, the annual meeting of the TESOL organization, was almost exclusively devoted to matters of classroom techniques and materials. These things are of course important and useful to teachers. What was lacking, however, was any sense of the sociopolitical contexts in which ELT is conducted, or of its role in those contexts.

To some extent these issues are now addressed both during the convention and in the year-round work of the TESOL organization (although I do not see this happening in many national ELT organizations). Over the last few years, for example, TESOL has kept an eye on potential legislature in the U. S. Congress that would affect the status of ESL students. However, even this is not quite what I mean. TESOL's advocacy efforts have to a large extent (perhaps unavoidably) focused on the needs of both child and adult

ESL learners: supporting bilingual education, for example, or fighting the English Only movement. From all I have seen, there is still no concerted effort to improve the lot of the teachers. Of course, TESOL is a professional organization and not a union. Nevertheless, because of the marginalization of the field (and also because of its great diversity), there seems to be no other organization that could strive to improve the working conditions of ESL and EFL teachers.

My message here is that in order to place a proper value on professional development in ELT we must take into account the sociopolitical conditions under which teachers work, and that advocacy must constitute an important part of work on teacher development. I believe we all bear a shared responsibility for working on this in whatever way we can. As a university-based teacher educator, I try to do my part in my courses and other work by raising my students' awareness of the sociopolitical dimensions of work in ELT and by making available to them information and resources regarding this aspect of the job. I would argue that administrators in language programs have a responsibility not just to ensure the best pay and working conditions they can for their teachers but to act in other ways: by not just tolerating but actively encouraging professional development, by advocating for teachers to their controlling authorities (B. Johnston & Peterson, 1994), and by introducing explicit hiring policies that do not discriminate against non-native speaker teachers so long as they have the necessary teaching abilities and language skills. Last, I call on teachers themselves to follow Bea's lead in taking themselves seriously as teachers—because, as she neatly puts it, "if *I* don't do things [...] nobody else is going to." It is only through our own efforts that the value of our work can become known and appreciated outside of ELT.

VALUES AND TEACHER EDUCATION

This book is addressed to practicing teachers, and so I have mostly kept away from the topic of teacher education. However, since I myself am both a teacher and a teacher educator, I hope you will allow me to indulge this dual role by saying at least a few words about how the preceding discussion relates to teacher education contexts, that is, formal programs in institutions of higher education in which teachers (usually, though by no means always, those with little or no prior teaching experience) formally study the teaching and learning of second languages.

For me, everything I have written thus far in this chapter and in the book as a whole applies to language teacher education just as much as it does to ELT. Teacher education is also teaching and, like other forms of teaching, it is rooted in values and in moral relations. It is for this reason that I have freely interspersed examples from my own work in teacher education amongst the examples from the work of EFL and ESL teachers.

As with ELT, with teacher education I believe that many of the prominent debates and dynamics in the field can be reconceptualized as debates about competing values. For example, there is something of an ongoing debate over the use of the terms *teacher training* and *teacher education* (Allwright, 2001). According to one version of this debate, *teacher training* is a narrower process involving primarily the acquisition of skills, whereas *researcher education* more widely addresses knowledge and dispositions as well (to use one common framework), that is, it "educates" the teacher in a deeper and more extensive way. This debate seems to me to reflect different values placed on the role of the teacher in the process of teacher learning and more generally extends to a different value placed on the teacher herself: as an implementer of pedagogical methods determined by others or as a vital and active participant in the processes of teaching and learning. The training–education distinction thus represents different values underlying the nature and purpose of teacher learning.

Another debate, which has become rather lively in the field of language teacher education, is that between the relative importance of pedagogical versus linguistic knowledge in teacher learning (Freeman & Johnson, 1998; K. E. Johnson & Freeman, 2001; Tarone & Allwright, 2001; Yates & Muchisky, 1999). To oversimplify, one side of this discussion suggests that in many teacher education programs there has been an overemphasis on decontextualized knowledge in such domains as linguistic theory and second language acquisition, and that what is needed is a greater stress on contextual understandings of actual classrooms and often non-linguistic aspects of teaching and learning (including both psychological factors, such as motivation, and especially sociocultural and sociopolitical factors). The other side contends that teachers need specialized knowledge about language and especially second language learning and that to purge language teacher education programs of courses in these topics is, as the expression goes, to throw the baby out with the bathwater.

I do not wish to adjudicate here between the two sides of this debate. What I would like to point out is that the debate itself seems to me to hinge on particular values assigned to the notion of "knowledge." The first side of the debate just described places greater value on contextual knowledge and thus both on practical matters and on the teacher–student relation. The other side, however, emphasizes the importance of abstract knowledge and abstract thinking and of the kinds of knowledge gained from formal research. As a researcher myself, I cannot be too quick to condemn this valuation of generalized knowledge, even as I feel my sympathies straying to the other side; this is all the more true because one important way in which teachers can improve their own standing is by learning to trade in the abstract discourse of the university. Regardless of where one stands on this issue, however, it is not merely a question of the structuring of a teacher education program but goes much deeper, to the values underlying that structure. Incidentally, it is also worth pointing out a far from trivial fact: that this same process automatically involves a valuing of the disciplines or subdisciplines of individual researchers and thus for them personally and professionally it is a moral matter. This is especially true because many faculty members in teacher education programs are specialists in areas such as second language acquisition or linguistic analysis; thus, the design of programs is not merely a technical question but a personal one for them (though of course this argument undercuts appeals sometimes made by these same faculty for rationality and objectivity in such decisions).

Thus, many of the underlying dynamics of language teacher education can be seen to be grounded in profoundly held yet contested values. There is another sense, though, in which teacher education is a moral undertaking. In teacher education, even more than in language teaching itself, there is a question of *integrity*, that is, the teacher educator has a double responsibility not only to guide students to becoming good or better teachers but also to be a good teacher herself. She must not only *tell* students how to teach well but must *show* them how. As Marshall McLuhan said in another context, the medium is the message.

Many teacher educators have made this same point. Woodward (1991), echoing the work of Argyris and Schön (1974), offered the notion of "loop input," in other words, using the teacher education classroom itself to demonstrate the kinds of techniques to which one is referring. If, for example, as a teacher educator you recommend to your students that they use pairwork, or journals, or process writing, instead of simply describing these things you can use them in your own classroom as a demonstration and to allow students to experience them first-hand. (The opposite of this, by the way, is exemplified by a certain faculty member I knew in my graduate education, who was famous for his half-hour lectures on reducing teacher talking time.)

Naturally, I agree wholeheartedly with the principle underlying Woodward's (1991) approach. My only quibble is that the notion of "loop input" itself seems to relegate the approach to the level of a set of techniques. For me, as I implied earlier, the matter at hand is above all a *moral* responsibility that we have as teacher educators (as suggested by the word *integrity*). A teacher educator who practices what she preaches is a "good" teacher educator not merely in the sense of an effective one but also in the sense that she is doing the good and right thing by her students. Conversely, the teacher educator who lectures, assigns multiple-choice examinations about teaching, and fails to develop a relationship with her students is not merely an ineffective teacher but in a broader sense is failing in her moral duty toward her students.

On the basis of these beliefs of mine, in my own work as a teacher educator I strive above all to teach in ways that I believe constitute good pedagogical practice. I do not claim always to be successful in this endeavor, but I have had sufficient feedback to know that I am at least moving in the right direction. I try to run my classes in a democratic manner, consulting students where choices of topic need to be made; I use dialogue journals and process writing, for reasons explained earlier; I individualize assignments by giving students the choice of topics; and I attempt to engage students in dialogue in class, not only by letting them speak but by encouraging them to expand on their views and by challenging them to think in new ways. Above all, I strive always to treat my students and their ideas with respect.

Last, there is an even deeper sense in which I hope to embody the values I hold. I mentioned that I do not give exams but instead use alternative forms of evaluation, such as portfolios. I always make a point of mentioning this explicitly to my students. However, what I really hope to convey to them is not that exams are bad but that it is vital that as teachers they think through choices such as what form of evaluation they will use, and that they can articulate and defend these choices to their own students. You may recall Professor O'Grady, my linguistics professor, whom I mentioned in chapter 4. O'Grady impressed me despite the fact that he used sit-down exams, because first he had thought through and could articulate the reasons for his choice, and second because he respected us, his students, enough to give us his explanation. It is this level of modeling, rather than a blind adherence to the particular techniques that I employ, that I hope to achieve. What matters is not that I use a particular set of approaches in my teaching but that I use them *for particular reasons*, and that those reasons are rooted in the values that I personally bring to class.

It is also at the level of values, rather than of particular techniques, that I hope to show other aspects of my teaching: respect for students; the courage to tackle difficult subjects; the intellectual clear-headedness needed to distinguish hard evidence from rhetoric. It is at this level, too, that I want to show professional development: The action research study on dialogue I described earlier served not only to gather information about that class but also to demonstrate tangibly to the members of the class what professional development can look like and, more generally than that, to show them the actions of a teacher committed to his own professional growth.

CONCLUSIONS

The one constant feature of all the aspects of teacher development mentioned in this chapter is change. It may be change in your job, change in your teaching practice, or change in your understanding of your own classroom, but without some kind of change there can be no development. Furthermore, just as our teaching of others is based on change for the better, so teacher development is predicated on change that leaves us better, in some way, than before. It is above all for this reason that teacher development is a moral process.

Not all teachers engage in the more time-consuming forms of teacher development such as TR; nor should they. In my view, it is imperative that teachers have control over their own professional development. If this means that they choose not to engage in TR, so be it. Yet all the good teachers I have known have engaged in *some* kind of professional development, although they may have avoided calling it that. They take on a new kind of class, design and use some new materials, or read a book about language teaching. All of these activities also constitute teacher development, and all should be appreciated for this reason. The important thing is that there should be change—or, to use a different image, movement—of some kind. On that note, I would end this chapter with a quotation from a poem by Thom Gunn called "On the Move," which I have long felt to capture the spirit of teacher development:

> At worst, one is in motion; and at best,
> Reaching no absolute, in which to rest,
> One is always nearer by not keeping still.
> (Gunn, 1967, p. 157)

QUESTIONS FOR REFLECTION AND DISCUSSION

1. Have you had any experience with any form of TR? If so, how was that experience? If not, would you be interested in trying out this kind of research in your own classroom? What values led you to your response to the previous question?

2. In the class which I describe in my study on dialogue, I was fortunate to have a small group of students, and so I had time to keep up a dialogue journal with each one. However, in many contexts teachers simply do not have the time or the resources to do this with every student. What other, less time-consuming ways are there to encourage the participation of shy students in the class? How can the needs of quiet students be met in large classes?

3. Look back at the description and analysis of Suzanne House's (in press) article about her volunteerism class. How might she have responded differently to the various conflicts of values that arose? How would you have handled this class differently, and what might you have said to the students? Do you think that the various objections raised by certain members of the class were cultural or individual in nature, or is this an oversimplification?

4. Reflect for a moment on your career in ELT. What have been the major turning points and decisions in your professional life? How have these related to your personal life? What values have guided you in choosing your career path? What conflicts of values have you experienced, and how have you tried to resolve them?

5. Think about your own teaching situation. Do you consider that you are marginalized in any way? If so, what forms does this marginalization take? What forms of advocacy are or would be useful in your situation?

6. In the section on marginality and advocacy I argued that teachers often undervalue their own professional knowledge. Do you agree with this idea? What aspects of your own professional knowledge are valued by you and by others around you, and which aspects are not appreciated? How might this state of affairs change?

7. Reflect on your own experiences in teacher education. Do you agree with my argument that teacher education, like teaching itself, is profoundly rooted in values? What kinds of values were evident in the teacher education programs you have known? What advice would you give to teacher educators in this regard?

7

Dilemmas and Foundations in English Language Teaching

In this book I have made a sustained argument for a view of language teaching as quintessentially grounded in values and moral beliefs. Specifically, I have argued that:

- All teaching is morally charged; that is, it is value-laden;
- Values are not simple and straightforward but complex and conflicting;
- Context is crucial in understanding the interplay of values in language classrooms—in other words, the interface between abstract, general values that we hold ("respect students,""be fair") and the things we say and do in the classroom is extremely complex and almost always indirect;
- Values exist at the meeting point between individual beliefs and those that are socially held or socially sanctioned.

In this final chapter I first gather together what seem to me to constitute the most important moral dilemmas (what Edge, 1996a, called "paradoxes") in English Language Teaching (ELT). I then consider the matter of moral foundations, given my repeated emphasis on the ambiguities, polyvalence, and the complexity of values and moral decision making. Finally, I revisit the teacher–student relation, the kernel of moral life in classrooms.

THE FUNDAMENTAL MORAL DILEMMAS OF ELT

Throughout this book I have used stories and examples of clashes of values experienced by actual teachers to exemplify common moral dilemmas faced by language teachers, and by teachers of English as a second or foreign language in particular. At this point I would like to bring many of these together. This is an attempt to expand on Edge's (1996a) identification of what he calls the central "paradoxes" of ELT. I have arranged these dilemmas into a rudimentary classification comprising three groups: dilemmas of pedagogy; dilemmas of teacher–student relations; and dilemmas of beliefs and values.

In my view, the most important moral dilemmas faced by professionals in ELT include the following:

Dilemmas of Pedagogy

1. Content versus form: How can I balance the need for a focus on language with the simultaneous need for language teaching to be about something meaningful? This is closely related to the paradox of communicative language teaching: The encouragement of "communication" can often mean the promotion of language production with little regard for the content of the communication taking place.

2. Process versus product: How do I socialize learners into accepted ways of writing and speaking while at the same time nurturing their ability to express themselves in ways authentic to themselves?

3. Voice and silence: How do I balance the right to speak with the right to be silent?

4. Evaluation: How do I evaluate my students, given the necessity of evaluation and the simultaneous impossibility of completely fair and objective methods?

5. Justification: At the broadest level, how do I justify the methods and techniques that I use, given that "science" will rarely if ever provide conclusive evidence of their effectiveness or otherwise?

Dilemmas of Teacher–Student Relations

6. Responsibility: To what extent should I exert my authority in order to force the learners to take responsibility for their learning, remembering that learners often resist this responsibility even though it is in their best interests (Woods, 1996)?

7. Authority versus solidarity: How can I balance the need to retain the authority and respect of the students with the need to maintain solidarity with them and "be on their side" (Barcelos, 2001; Feiman-Nemser & Floden, 1986)?
8. Institutionality: How can I balance my position as individual and as teacher with my *de facto* role as representative of the institution in which I work?

Dilemmas of Beliefs and Values

9. Politics: As best expressed by Edge (1996a), "to be involved in TESOL anywhere is to be involved in issues of liberation and domination everywhere" (p. 17). How do I reconcile this fact with the positive values that we carry as ELT professionals?
10. Personal faith: In what ways, and to what extent, should my religious and spiritual beliefs directly or indirectly influence my work in language classrooms?
11. Tolerance: If I embrace tolerance as a value, how am I to respond to intolerance expressed by others in my classroom?
12. Professionalism: How can I reconcile the identity of being a professional with the realities of ELT in most countries and contexts?

Of course, this classification is only really a conceptual aid. All these dilemmas affect our pedagogy. All influence the teacher–student relation. And first and foremost, all are rooted in profound clashes of values and beliefs that we hold as teachers. However these dilemmas are classified, though, taken together they convey some of the complexity of the moral landscape of the ELT classroom.

THE SEARCH FOR FOUNDATIONS

Throughout this book, I have stressed that because of the complex moral topography of the classroom, decisions made by teachers are never straightforward but always at some level involve a clash of values. In this section I underline the fact that, although I believe this is so, I also believe firmly in the possibility of adjudicating in most situations between better and worse courses of action, based on a given teacher's values.

Though I have not concealed my own beliefs and views in what I have written, I have repeatedly emphasized the fact that every teacher will have a different view of the moral dilemmas of classroom life. Nevertheless, I believe there are certain foundational issues that must be acknowledged if we are first to understand the moral contours of classrooms, and second to avoid moral paralysis (Applebaum, 1996) in the face of uncertainty and ambiguity.

First and foremost, I believe strongly that each teacher has a moral duty to examine her own values and beliefs about what is good and right for her own learners. I see this as a responsibility of the teacher, one that comes from the corresponding right to make her own decisions about values. Socrates said that "the unexamined life is not worth living." While I might not go so far, I do believe that teachers should continue to reflect on their own values and on the ways in which these values are reflected or denied in their practice (Whitehead, 1993).

Second, despite everything I have said about the complexity and ambiguity of the teacher's moral decision making, I believe that there are some actions that are clearly more morally defensible than others—that is, in many cases there does exist a course of action that is right and good for the learners. I believe that testing that tries to catch students out in what they do not know instead of encouraging them to display what they do know is unequivocally wrong. I believe that in almost every case, flexibility in matters such as deadlines and requirements is better than unbending adherence to rules. I believe that there should always be room for student input into the structure and management of classes. I believe that any course of instruction that places the material above the learners—that, for example, expects teachers and students to move in lockstep fashion through a course book at a predetermined rate—is fundamentally misguided.

Of course, you may disagree with me on some of these points. However, from my own perspective, and for all my doubts, these are working moral absolutes, and in my own teaching and work in teacher education I do all I can to enact such values in my classroom and to encourage (but not force) other teachers to adopt them.

Third, it is clear to me that the kinds of judgments I have just passed arise from certain key values that I hold yet that are not peculiar to me alone but are shared by many in our field. Edge (1996a) identified some of these values: diversity, inquiry, cooperation, respect (p. 12). I would add: commitment to our students, commitment to ourselves, equity, caring, and dialogue as fundamental values underlying our pedagogical beliefs. Though, as I pointed out earlier, the complexity of actual situations renders the relationship between these values and our actions equally complex, it is vital that we see such values as triangulation points in the processes of moral decision making.

Last, despite my (lack of) religious beliefs (see chap. 5), I do believe in the existence of moral absolutes, and I believe that my beliefs are shared by a great many teachers in ELT. I believe in the absolute and unconditional equality of men and women. I believe in the absolute and unconditional equality of people of all races. I believe that individuals should have control over their own actions. In conflicts between those with power and those without, I believe that we have a moral duty to try to understand the viewpoint of those without power. Such beliefs occasionally bring me into conflict with others—when I conducted some workshops recently in Turkey, for example, my extremely gracious Turkish hosts were, shall we say, troubled when I tried to represent the Kurdish point of view to them. In connection with this, I certainly do not believe in thrusting these views down the throats of others. However, I do regard them, to adapt Edge's (1996a) phrase, as moral bedrock.

I do not believe in imposing my views on others. Indeed, that would be a literally impossible task, because the whole point about such views is that they are privately, individually held. Furthermore, as I mentioned in chapter 1, such views are also ultimately beyond the reach of logic. I think that all I can do is attempt to live my views in my teaching and to write about them, for instance, in this book. My point is not that these are the only moral certainties but that moral absolutes can and do exist.

In fact, though this may be something of an aside, I would go further. Many of the views I just expressed, although not accepted by all individuals or all governments, have in fact been quasi-legally encoded in documents such as the *Universal Declaration of Human Rights* (1948). Many people have castigated the 20th century as an age of unrivaled brutality and violence, from the pitiless slaughter of the First World War, through Hitler's death camps and Stalin's purges, to the killing fields of Cambodia, Rwanda, and Bosnia at end of century. This history is, of course, undeniable. Yet I do see a ray of hope. The 20th century was also the age in which the human race as a whole, often through the United Nations and similar organizations, finally came to certain moral conclusions: Equality between the races and equality between men and women are two clear examples. Though the political realities often lag woefully behind, the fact is that in 1900 it was morally acceptable to argue the inequality of women or non-Whites, whereas in 2000 such arguments are no longer taken seriously—they are morally bankrupt. While politically there is a huge distance to go, it does seem to me that, morally speaking, we have taken a significant step forward. For this reason, I feel justified in being hopeful that the beliefs I have expressed here are not merely my own idiosyncratic views but reflect more universally held values with which the field of ELT as a whole will identify.[1]

THE TEACHER–STUDENT RELATION REVISITED

I end by taking a last look at the teacher–student relation, since in many ways this relation forms the backbone of this book.

I hope it is clear from what I have written here that in saying that the teacher–student relation is the most important component of language teaching I am *not* advocating chummy, touchy–feely friendships with all one's students. An important part of my message has been that each teacher negotiates the particulars of relations with students in different ways, and that this is as it should be. Some teachers socialize with their students; others disappear at the end of the day and reappear the next morning. Neither practice is inherently right or wrong. I certainly do not believe that teachers have a duty to extend the teacher–student relation beyond the school.

My point, rather, is that *however* the teacher–student relation is played out, it is the moral foundation of teaching. Wherever and whenever we encounter students—in the classroom, in our offices, or elsewhere—we are meeting with them above all as one human with another, and our treatment of them is thus always a moral matter. This is only compounded by the additional fact that in the vast majority of cases we hold a position of higher status and power than our learners—that we are not encountering them as equals (Noddings, 1984). This simply places a greater moral burden on our shoulders to ensure that our own contribution to the teacher–student relation is morally grounded.

I also wish to emphasize once again that each teacher–student relation is unique and must be treated as such. This is precisely why the quest

---

[1] I debated with myself for a long time over whether to refer here to the events of September 11, 2001, which took place between the preparation of the first and second drafts of this book. As you can see, I have compromised by mentioning them in a footnote. Terrible as those events were, I do not believe that they offer any argument against the moral universals that, I suggest, emerged over the course of the last century. From my perspective, the terrorist acts of September 11 are merely a particularly evil continuation of the 20th-century atrocities mentioned earlier. The fact that they were carried out in such a prominent place on the world stage does not make them inherently different from many other terrible examples of human cruelty that recent history has seen. For this reason, while condemning the attacks, and the ideologies behind them that not only condone but also promote such acts, I cannot see that they in any way detract from the gradual historical emergence of the universally agreed-on values encoded, for instance, in the Universal Declaration of Human Rights.

for justice and equity in the classroom is so phenomenally difficult: Learners are never comparable, and the more we meet them as individuals (as we should), the harder it is to compare them to one another, whether in test scores, the time we devote to them, or whatever. In any case, I whole-heartedly agree with Ayers (1993) when he argued that it is neither possible nor desirable to treat all learners "the same" (p. 12). Rather, with each new learner I must figure out the details of the teacher–student relation, with only partial guidance available from the abstract values I espouse and from my previous encounters with other, different students.

In fact, I would argue that although equity is a core value, it is often achieved precisely by treating students differently rather than by striving to treat them all in the same way. I spend much more time with some students than with others—remember how much time I devoted to Hae-young (chap. 1), for example. I cut some students more slack than others. I even force myself to be strict and firm with some students *if I believe that such treatment is in the best interests of those students.* I like some students more than others. To some students I give especial encouragement, either because they need it, or because they show particular promise, or both. All these things, I argue, are a natural part of teaching and a natural consequence of what Noddings (1984) called "the uniqueness of human encounters" (p. 5).

This last notion is a reminder that all values and moral dilemmas are played out in encounters between a particular teacher and a particular student at a particular moment in time. For this reason, I have deliberately chosen to exemplify my points in this book with stories about actual teachers taken from real life. It seems to me that in exploring the moral contours of classrooms, narrative ways of knowing (K. E. Johnson & Golombek, in press; Witherell & Noddings, 1991) are the most appropriate and the most useful. For the same reason, I want to end my book not with a summative statement but with a story, this time from a class in phonology I taught a few years ago.

One day in this class I presented the structure of the syllable in English—onset, rhyme, coda and so on. After the class a Taiwanese student named Ling came up to me and said: "You know what, I don't think we have syllables in Chinese." Quite instinctively, but on the basis of my relation with Ling, who was an enthusiastic and friendly student, I responded not with categorical certainty—"Of course you do!"—but in a much gentler way. I said, "You know, I think you do." Ling replied: "No, I'm pretty sure we don't." I paused. "You know what," I said. "In four weeks you have a paper due on some aspect of phonology. Why don't you go and research this and write your paper on whether Chinese has syllables or not?" Ling eagerly agreed. A few days later, after clearly having spent some time in the library, she came up to me after class again, this time grinning delightedly. "Guess what?" she said. "Chinese does have syllables after all!" And she wrote me an excellent paper on the syllable structure of Mandarin Chinese.

The reason I love this story is not only that it shows how teacher and student can collaborate in helping the student to discover learning for herself, but also that, more broadly, it captures a successful instance of the way in which learning takes place as a result of the particular relation between teacher and learner, and their respective contributions to it, in a very specific context in time and space. It is this kind of discovery that offers me the strongest confirmation of the centrality of the student–teacher relation in our work as teachers.

References

Allwright, D. (2001). Three major processes of teacher development and the appropriate design criteria for developing and using them. In B. Johnston & S. Irujo (Eds.), *Research and practice in language teacher education: Voices from the field* (pp. 115–133). Minneapolis: University of Minnesota, Center for Advanced Research in Second Language Acquisition.

Allwright, D., & Lenzuen, R. (1997). Exploratory practice: Work at the Cultura Inglesa, Rio de Janeiro, Brazil. *Language Teaching Research, 1,* 73–79.

Amirault, C. (1995). The good teacher, the good student: Identifications of a student teacher. In J. Gallop (Ed.), *Pedagogy: The question of impersonation* (pp. 64–78). Bloomington: Indiana University Press.

Applebaum, B. (1996). Moral paralysis and the ethnocentric fallacy. *Journal of Moral Education, 25,* 185–199.

Argyris, C., & Schön, D. A. (1974). *Theory in practice: Increasing professional effectiveness.* San Francisco: Jossey-Bass.

Aristotle (1926). *The Nicomachean ethics* (H. Rackham, trans.). Cambridge, MA: Harvard University Press.

Auerbach, E. R. (1993). Reexamining English Only in the ESL classroom. *TESOL Quarterly, 27,* 9–32.

Auerbach, E. R., & Paxton, D. (1997). "It's not the English thing": Bringing reading research into the ESL classroom. *TESOL Quarterly, 31,* 237–261.

Auerbach, E. R., & Wallerstein, N. (1987). *ESL for action: Problem-posing at work.* Reading, MA: Addison-Wesley.

Ayers, W. (1993). *To teach: The journey of a teacher.* New York: Teachers College Press.

Bachman, L. F. (2000). Modern language testing at the turn of the century: Assuring that what we count counts. *Language Testing, 17,* 1–42.

Bailey, K. M., & Nunan, D. (Eds.). (1996). *Voices from the language classroom.* Cambridge, England: Cambridge University Press.

Bakhtin, M. M. (1981). *The dialogic imagination* (C. Emerson & M. Holquist, trans.). Austin: University of Texas Press.

Ball, D. L., & Wilson, S. M. (1996). Integrity in teaching: Recognizing the fusion of the moral and intellectual. *American Educational Research Journal, 33*, 155–192.

Ball, S. J. (Ed.). (1990). *Foucault and education: Disciplines and knowledge.* London: Routledge.

Barcelos, A. M. (2001). The interaction between students' beliefs and teacher's beliefs and dilemmas. In B. Johnston & S. Irujo (Eds.), *Research and practice in language teacher education: Voices from the field* (pp. 77–97). Minneapolis: University of Minnesota, Center for Advanced Research in Second Language Acquisition.

Bauman, Z. (1993). *Postmodern ethics.* Cambridge, MA: Blackwell.

Bauman, Z. (1994). *Alone again: Ethics after certainty.* London: Demos.

Bauman, Z. (1995). *Life in fragments: Essays in postmodern morality.* Oxford, England: Blackwell.

Benesch, S. (1993). ESL, ideology, and the politics of pragmatism. *TESOL Quarterly, 27*, 705–717.

Bentham, J. (1948). *An introduction to the principles of morals and legislation.* New York: Hafner. (Original work published 1789)

Bergem, T. (1990). The teacher as moral agent. *Journal of Moral Education, 19*, 88–100.

Boshell, M. (in press). What I learned from giving quiet children space. In K. E. Johnson & P. R. Golombek (Eds.), *Teachers' ways of knowing: Narrative inquiry as professional development.* Cambridge, England: Cambridge University Press.

Bowers, B., & Godfrey, J. (1985). *Decisions, decisions.* Agincourt, Ontario, Canada: Dominie.

Branscombe, N. A., Goswami, D., & Schwartz, J. (1992). *Students teaching, teachers learning.* Portsmouth, NH: Boynton/Cook Heinemann.

Breen, M. P. (1984). Process syllabuses for the classroom. In C. J. Brumfit (Ed.), *General English syllabus design: Curriculum and syllabus design for the general English classroom* (pp. 47–60). Oxford, England: Pergamon.

Brown, H. D. (1994). *Teaching by principles. An interactive approach to language pedagogy.* Upper Saddle River, NJ: Prentice Hall Regents.

Burns, A. (1999). *Collaborative action research for English language teachers.* Cambridge, England: Cambridge University Press.

Buzzelli, C. A., & Johnston, B. (2002). *The moral dimensions of teaching: Language, power, and culture in classroom interaction.* New York: Routledge Falmer.

Byrnes, H., & Canale, M. (Eds.). (1987). *Defining and developing proficiency: Guidelines, implementations and concepts.* Lincolnwood, IL: National Textbook.

Canagarajah, S. (1993). Critical ethnography of a Sri Lankan classroom: Ambiguities in opposition to reproduction through TESOL. *TESOL Quarterly, 27*, 601–626.

Centre for British Teachers. (1989). *Pilot study of the career paths of EFL teachers.* Reading, England: Author.

Cole, D. J., Ryan, C. W., & Kick, F. (1995). *Portfolios across the curriculum and beyond.* Thousand Oaks, CA: Corwin.

Coleman, H. (Ed.). (1996). *Society and the language classroom.* Cambridge, England: Cambridge University Press.

Colnerud, G. (1997). Ethical conflicts in teaching. *Teaching and Teacher Education, 13,* 627–635.

Court Upholds Firing Over Refusal to Change Grade. (2001, April 20). *Herald Times,* (Bloomington), p. A5.

Crookes, G., & Lehner, A. (1998). Aspects of process in an ESL critical pedagogy teacher education course. *TESOL Quarterly, 32,* 319–328.

De Fina, A. A. (1992). *Portfolio assessment: Getting started.* New York: Scholastic.

Delpit, L. (1995). *Other people's children: Cultural conflict in the classroom.* New York: New Press.

Dewey, J. (1909). *Moral principles in education.* Boston: Houghton Mifflin.

Duff, P. A., & Uchida, Y. (1997). The negotiation of teachers' sociocultural identities and practices in postsecondary EFL classrooms. *TESOL Quarterly, 31,* 451–486.

DuFon, M. (1993). Ethics in TESOL research. *TESOL Quarterly, 27,* 157–160.

Eastman, C. M. (1990). What is the role of language planning in post-apartheid South Africa? *TESOL Quarterly, 24,* 9–21.

Edge, J. (1992). *Cooperative development.* Harlow, England: Longman.

Edge, J. (1996a). Cross-cultural paradoxes in a profession of values. *TESOL Quarterly, 30,* 9–30.

Edge, J. (1996b). Keeping the faith. *TESOL Matters, 6*(4), 1.

Edge, J. (Ed.). (2001a). *Action research.* Alexandria, VA: TESOL.

Edge, J. (2001b). Attitude and access: Building a new teaching/learning community in TESOL. In J. Edge (Ed.), *Action research* (pp. 1–11). Alexandria, VA: TESOL.

Edge, J. (2001c, May). *Build it and they will come.* Plenary address presented at the Second International Conference on Language Teacher Education, Minneapolis, MN.

Edge, J. (2002). *Continuing cooperative development. A discourse framework for individuals as colleagues.* Ann Arbor: University of Michigan Press.

Edge, J., & Richards, K. (Eds.). (1993). *Teachers develop teachers research.* Oxford, England: Heinemann.

Edstam, T. S. (2001). Perceptions of professionalism among elementary school ESL teachers. In B. Johnston & S. Irujo (Eds.), *Research and practice in language teacher education: Voices from the field* (pp. 233–249). Minneapolis: University of Minnesota, Center for Advanced Research in Second Language Acquisition.

Eisenberg, J. A. (1992). *The limits of reason: Indeterminacy in law, education, and morality.* New Brunswick, NJ: Transaction.

Elbow, P. (1973). *Writing without teachers*. Oxford, England: Oxford University Press.

Emig, J. (1971). *The composing processes of twelfth graders*. Urbana, IL: National Council of Teachers of English.

Ewald, J. D. (2001). *Listening to learners' and teachers' voices: Pedagogical theory encounters reality in collaborative group work in the language classroom*. Unpublished doctoral dissertation, University of Minnesota.

Feiman-Nemser, S., & Floden, R. E. (1986). The cultures of teaching. In M. Wittrock (Ed.), *Handbook of research on teaching* (pp. 505–526). New York: Macmillan.

Finocchiaro, M., & Brumfit, C. J. (1983). *The functional–notional approach: From theory to practice*. Oxford, England: Oxford University Press.

Fishman, J. (1991). *Reversing language shift*. Clevedon: Multilingual Matters.

Foucault, M. (1972). *The archeology of knowledge* (A. M. Sheridan Smith, trans.). New York: Pantheon.

Foucault, M. (1978). *The care of the self* (A. Sheridan, trans.). New York: Vintage.

Foucault, M. (1979). *Discipline and punish: The birth of the prison* (A. Sheridan, trans.). New York: Vintage.

Foucault, M. (1980). *Power/knowledge: Selected interviews and other writings of Michel Foucault* (C. Gordon, Ed.). Brighton, England: Harvester.

Freeman, D. (1998). *Doing teacher-research: From inquiry to understanding*. Pacific Grove, CA: Heinle & Heinle.

Freeman, D., & Johnson, K. E. (1998). Reconceptualizing the knowledge-base of language teacher education. *TESOL Quarterly, 32*, 397–417.

Freire, P. (1972). *Pedagogy of the oppressed* (M. B. Ramos, trans.). London: Penguin.

Frye, D. (1999). Participatory education as a critical framework for an immigrant women's ESL class. *TESOL Quarterly, 33*, 501–513.

Gee, J. P. (1990). *Social linguistics and literacies: Ideology in discourses*. London: Falmer.

Genesee, F., & Upshur, J. A. (1996). *Classroom-based evaluation in second language education*. Cambridge, England: Cambridge University Press.

Gergen, K. J. (1991). *The saturated self: Dilemmas of identity in everyday life*. New York: Basic Books.

Gert, B. (1988). *Morality: A new justification of the moral rules*. New York: Oxford University Press.

Gert, B. (1998). *Morality: Its nature and justification*. New York: Oxford University Press.

Giddens, A. (2000). *Runaway world: How globalization is shaping our lives*. New York: Routledge.

Gipps, C., & Murphy, P. (1994). *A fair test? Assessment, achievement and equity*. Buckingham, England: Open University Press.

Giroux, H. A. (1988). *Teachers as intellectuals: Towards a critical pedagogy of learning*. Granby, MA: Bergin and Garvey.

Giroux, H. A. (1991). Modernism, postmodernism, and feminism: Rethinking the boundaries of educational discourse. In H. A. Giroux (Ed.), *Postmodernism, feminism and cultural politics: Redrawing educational boundaries* (pp. 1–59). Albany: State University of New York Press.

Goodlad, J. I., Soder, R., & Sirotnik, K. A. (Eds.). (1990). *The moral dimensions of teaching*. San Francisco: Jossey-Bass.

Goodman, Y. (1985). Kidwatching: Observing children in the classroom. In A. Jaggar & M. T. Smith-Burke (Eds.), *Observing the language learner* (pp. 9–18). Newark, DE: International Reading Association.

Gunn, T. (1967). On the move. In A. Alvarez (Ed.), *The new poetry* (pp. 156–157). Harmondsworth, England: Penguin.

Hadley, G., & Evans, C. (2001). Constructions across a culture gap. In J. Edge (Ed.), *Action research* (pp. 129–143). Alexandria, VA: TESOL.

Hafernik, J., Messerschmitt, D. S., & Vandrick, S. (in press). *Ethical issues for ESL faculty: Social justice issues in practice*. Mahwah, NJ: Lawrence Erlbaum Associates.

Hall, J. K., & Eggington, W. G. (Eds.). (2000). *The sociopolitics of English language teaching*. Clevedon, England: Multilingual Matters.

Halliday, M. A. K. (1978). *Language as social semiotic: The social interpretation of language and meaning*. Baltimore: University Park Press.

Hamp-Lyons, L. (1998). Ethical test preparation practice: The case of the TOEFL. *TESOL Quarterly, 32*, 329–337.

Hansen, D. T. (1993). From role to person: The moral layeredness of classroom teaching. *American Educational Research Journal, 30*, 651–674.

Hargreaves, A. (1994). *Changing teachers, changing times: Teachers' work and culture in the postmodern age*. New York: Teachers College Press.

Harklau, L. (2000). From the "good kids" to the "worst": Representations of English language learners across educational settings. *TESOL Quarterly, 34*, 35–67.

Harman, G., & Thomson, J. J. (1996). *Moral relativism and moral objectivity*. Cambridge, MA: Blackwell.

Herman, J. L., Aschbacher, P. R., & Winters, L. (1992). *A practical guide to alternative assessment*. Alexandria, VA: Association for Supervision and Curriculum Development.

Hill, B. V. (1991). *Values education in Australian schools*. Melbourne, Australia: ACER.

Holland, D., Lachicotte, W., Skinner, D., & Cain, C. (1998). *Identity and agency in cultural worlds*. Cambridge, MA: Harvard University Press.

Horowitz, D. M. (1986). What professors actually require: Academic tasks for the ESL classroom. *TESOL Quarterly, 20*, 445–462.

House, S. (in press). Who is in this classroom with me? In K. E. Johnson & P. R. Golombek (Eds.), *Teachers' ways of knowing: Narrative inquiry as professional development*. Cambridge, England: Cambridge University Press.

Hutchinson, T., & Torres, E. (1994). The textbook as agent of change. *English Language Teaching Journal, 48,* 315–328.

Igoa, C. (1995). *The inner world of the immigrant child*. New York: St. Martin's Press.

Irujo, S. (2000). A process syllabus in a methodology course: Experiences, beliefs, challenges. In M. P. Breen & A. Littlejohn (Eds.), *Classroom decision-making: Negotiation and process syllabuses in practice* (pp. 209–222). Cambridge, England: Cambridge University Press.

Jackson, P. W., Boostrom, R. E., & Hansen, D. T. (1993). *The moral life of schools*. San Francisco: Jossey-Bass.

Janangelo, J. (1993). To serve, with love: Liberation theory and the mystification of teaching. In P. Kahaney, L . A. M. Perry, & J. Janangelo (Eds.), *Theoretical and critical perspectives on teacher change* (pp. 134–150). Norwood, NJ: Ablex.

Jaworski, A. (1992). *The power of silence: Social and pragmatic perspectives*. Newbury Park, CA: Sage.

Johnson K. A. (in press). Action for understanding: A study in teacher research with exploratory practice. In K. E. Johnson & P. R. Golombek (Eds.), *Teachers' ways of knowing: Narrative inquiry as professional development*. Cambridge, England: Cambridge University Press.

Johnson, K. E., & Freeman, D. (2001, May). *Towards linking teacher knowledge and student learning*. Plenary address presented at the Second International Conference on Language Teacher Education, Minneapolis, MN.

Johnson, K. E., & Golombek, P. R. (Eds.). (in press). *Teachers' ways of knowing: Narrative inquiry as professional development*. Cambridge, England: Cambridge University Press.

Johnston, B. (1997). Do EFL teachers have careers? *TESOL Quarterly, 31,* 681–712.

Johnston, B. (1999a). The expatriate teacher as postmodern paladin. *Research in the Teaching of English, 34,* 255–280.

Johnston, B. (1999b). Putting critical pedagogy in its place: A personal account. *TESOL Quarterly, 33,* 557–565.

Johnston, B. (2000). Investigating dialogue in language teacher education: The teacher educator as learner. In K. E. Johnson (Ed.), *Teacher education* (pp. 157–173). Alexandria, VA: TESOL.

Johnston, B. (in press). The rise and fall of a Dakota immersion pre-school. *Journal of Multilingual and Multicultural Development*.

Johnston, B., & Buzzelli, C. A. (2002). Expressive morality: A case study in the creation of moral meaning through classroom discourse. *Language and Education, 16,* 37–47.

Johnston, B., & Goettsch, K. (2000). In search of the knowledge base of language teaching: Explanations by experienced teachers. *Canadian Modern Language Review, 56,* 437–468.

Johnston, B., Juhász, A., Marken, J., & Ruiz, B. R. (1998). The ESL teacher as moral agent. *Research in the Teaching of English, 32,* 161–181.

Johnston, B., Mahan-Taylor, R., & Pawan, F. (2001, May). *The professional development of working ESL/EFL teachers.* Paper presented at the Second International Conference on Language Teacher Education, Minneapolis, MN.

Johnston, B., & Peterson, S. (1994). The program matrix: A conceptual framework for language programs. *System, 22,* 63–80.

Johnston, B., Ruiz, B. R., & Juhász, A. (2002). *The moral dimension of ESL classroom interaction: Multiple perspectives on critical moral incidents.* Manuscript submitted for publication.

Johnston, D. K. (1991). Cheating: Reflections on a moral dilemma. *Journal of Moral Education, 20,* 283–291.

Joseph, P. B., & Ephron, S. (1993). Moral choices/moral conflicts: Teachers' self-perceptions. *Journal of Moral Education, 22,* 201–220.

Katz, A. (2000). Changing paradigms for assessment. In M. A. Snow (Ed.), *Implementing the ESL standards for Pre-K–12 students through teacher education* (pp. 137–166). Alexandria, VA: TESOL.

Katz, M. S., Noddings, N., & Strike, K. A. (Eds.). (1999). *Justice and caring: The search for common ground in education.* New York: Teachers College Press.

Krashen, S. (1981). *Second language acquisition and second language learning.* Oxford, England: Pergamon.

Krauss, M. (1992). The world's languages in crisis. *Language, 68,* 4–10.

Kristeva, J. (1984). *Revolution in poetic language* (L. Roudiez, trans.). New York: Columbia University Press.

Kumaravadivelu, B. (1994). The postmethod condition: (E)merging strategies for second/foreign language teaching. *TESOL Quarterly, 28,* 27–48.

Li, X. (1999). Writing from the vantage point of an outsider/insider. In G. Braine (Ed.), *Non-native educators in English language teaching* (pp. 43–55). Mahwah, NJ: Lawrence Erlbaum Associates.

Ling, L., & Stephenson, J. (1998). Introduction and theoretical perspectives. In J. Stephenson, L. Ling, E. Burman, & M. Cooper (Eds.), *Values in education* (pp. 3–19). London: Routledge.

Machado, A. (1941). *Poesías completas* (Collected Poems) (5th ed.). Madrid, Spain: Espasa-Calpe.

MacLure, M. (1993). Arguing for your self: Identity as an organizing principle in teachers' jobs and lives. *British Educational Research Journal, 19,* 311–322.

Maley, A. (1992). An open letter to "the profession." *English Language Teaching Journal, 46,* 96–99.

Maslow, A. H. (1959). *New knowledge in human values.* New York: Harper.

Maxwell, M. (1991). *Moral inertia: Ideas for social action.* Niwot, CO: University Press of Colorado.

McElroy-Johnson, B. (1993). Giving voice to the voiceless. *Harvard Educational Review, 63,* 85–104.

McKnight, A. (1992). "I loved the course, but ... " Career aspirations and realities in adult TESOL. *Prospect, 7*(3), 20–31.

McLaren, P. (1989). *Life in schools: An introduction to critical pedagogy in the foundations of education.* New York: Longman.

McLaughlin, D., & Tierney, W. G. (1993). *Naming silenced lives: Personal narratives and processes of educational change.* New York: Routledge.

McNamara, T. (1996). *Measuring second language performance.* London: Longman.

Mehrens, W. A., & Kaminsky, J. (1989). Methods for improving standardized test scores: Fruitful, fruitless, or fraudulent? *Educational Measurement: Issues and Practice, 8*(1), 14–22.

Middleton, S. (1998). *Disciplining sexuality: Foucault, life histories, and education.* New York: Teachers College Press.

Mill, J. S. (1998). *Utilitarianism.* Oxford, England: Oxford University Press. (Original work published 1863)

Milton, O., Pollio, H. R., & Eison, J. A. (1986). *Making sense of college grades.* San Francisco: Jossey-Bass.

Mittelman, J. H. (2000). *The globalization syndrome: Transformation and resistance.* Princeton, NJ: Princeton University Press.

Morgan, B. (1997). Identity and intonation: Linking dynamic processes in an ESL classroom. *TESOL Quarterly, 31,* 431–450.

Morgan, B. D. (1998). *The ESL classroom: Teaching, critical practice, and community development.* Toronto, Ontario, Canada: University of Toronto Press.

Murray, D. (1982). *Learning by teaching: Selected articles on writing and teaching.* Upper Montclair, NJ: Boynton Cook.

Noblit, G. W., & Dempsey, V. O. (1996). *The social construction of virtue: The moral life of schools.* Albany: State University of New York Press.

Noddings, N. (1984). *Caring: A feminine approach to ethics and moral education.* Berkeley: University of California Press.

Noddings, N. (1992). *The challenge to care in schools.* New York: Teachers College Press.

Norton, B. (1997). Language, identity, and the ownership of English. *TESOL Quarterly, 31,* 409–429.

Norton Peirce, B. (1995). Social identity, investment, and language learning. *TESOL Quarterly, 29,* 9–31.

Nunan, D. (1988). *The learner-centered curriculum.* Cambridge, England: Cambridge University Press.

Nunan, D. (1989). *Understanding language classrooms. A guide for teacher-initiated action.* Englewood Cliffs, NJ: Prentice Hall.

Nunan, D. (1999a). So you think that language teaching is a profession (Part I). *TESOL Matters, 9*(4).

Nunan, D. (1996b) So you think that language teaching is a profession (Part II). *TESOL Matters, 9*(5).

Oderberg, D. S. (2000). *Moral theory: A non-consequentialist approach.* Oxford, England: Blackwell.

O'Malley, J. M., & Valdez Pierce, L. (1996). *Authentic assessment for English language learners: Practical approaches for teachers.* New York: Addison-Wesley.

Pawlik, C., & Stumpfhauser de Hernandez, A. (1995). *Freeway: An integrated course in communicative English. Student book 2.* Harlow: Longman.

Pennington, M. C. (1992). Second class or economy? The status of the English language teaching profession in tertiary education. *Prospect, 7*(3), 7–19.

Pennycook, A. (1989). The concept of method, interested knowledge, and the politics of language teaching. *TESOL Quarterly, 23,* 589–618.

Pennycook, A. (1994). *The cultural politics of English as an international language.* London: Longman.

Pennycook, A. (1996). Borrowing others' words: Ownership, memory, and plagiarism. *TESOL Quarterly, 30,* 201–230.

Pennycook, A. (2001). *Critical applied linguistics: A critical introduction.* Mahwah, NJ: Lawrence Erlbaum Associates.

Phillipson, R. (1992). *Linguistic imperialism.* Oxford, England: Oxford University Press.

Placier, M. (1996). An action research approach to a contradiction in teaching: Reconciling grades with democratic education. *Action in Teacher Education, 18*(3), 23–32.

Popham, W. J. (1991). Appropriateness of teachers' test-preparation practices. *Educational Measurement: Issues and Practice, 10*(4), 12–15.

Popkewitz, T. S. (1994). Professionalization in teaching and teacher education: Some notes on its history, ideology, and potential. *Teaching and Teacher Education, 10,* 1–14.

Popkewitz, T. S., & Brennan, M. (Eds.). (1998). *Foucault's challenge: Discourse, knowledge, and power in education.* New York: Teachers College Press.

Power, F. C., & Lapsley, D. K. (Eds.) (1992). *The challenge of pluralism: Education, politics, and values.* South Bend, IN: University of Notre Dame Press.

Powers, D. E., Schedl, M. A., & Wilson, S. (1999). Validating the Test of Spoken English against a criterion of communicative success. *Language Testing, 16,* 399–425.

Prabhu, N. S. (1990). There is no best method—Why? *TESOL Quarterly, 24,* 161–176.

Rachels, J. (1998). Introduction. In J. Rachels (Ed.), *Ethical theory* (pp.1–33). Oxford, England: Oxford University Press.

Raimes, A. (1991). Out of the woods: Emerging traditions in the teaching of writing. *TESOL Quarterly, 25,* 407–430.

Rawls, J. (1971). *A theory of justice*. Cambridge, MA: Harvard University Press.

Rea-Dickins, P., & Gardner, S. (2000). Snares or silver bullets: Disentangling the construct of formative assessment. *Language Testing, 17,* 215–243.

Richard-Amato, P. A. (1996). *Making it happen: Interaction in the second language classroom* (2nd ed.). White Plains, NY: Longman.

Rivera, K. M. (1999). Popular research and social transformation: A community-based approach to critical pedagogy. *TESOL Quarterly, 33,* 485–500.

Rogers, J. (1982). "The world for sick proper." *English Language Teaching Journal, 36,* 144–151.

Sarup, M. (1996). *Identity, culture, and the postmodern world*. Athens: University of Georgia Press.

Scollon, R., & Wong Scollon, S. (1995). *Intercultural communication: A discourse approach*. Malden, MA: Blackwell.

Shohamy, E. (1998). Critical language testing and beyond. *Studies in Educational Evaluation, 24,* 331–345.

Shor, I. (1996). *When students have power: Negotiating authority in a critical pedagogy*. Chicago: University of Chicago Press.

Schrag, C. O. (1997). *The self after postmodernity*. New Haven, CT: Yale University Press.

Shulman, L. S. (1987). Knowledge and teaching: Foundations of the new reform. *Harvard Educational Review, 57,* 1–22.

Silva, T. (1997). On the ethical treatment of ESL writers. *TESOL Quarterly, 31,* 359–363.

Simpson, P. J., & Garrison, J. (1995). Teaching and moral perception. *Teachers College Record, 97,* 252–278.

Skutnabb-Kangas, T. (2000). *Linguistic genocide in education or worldwide diversity and human rights?* Mahwah, NJ: Lawrence Erlbaum Associates.

Sockett, H. (1993). *The moral base of teacher professionalism*. New York: Teachers College Press.

Spring, J. (1998). *Education and the rise of the global economy*. Mahwah, NJ: Lawrence Erlbaum Associates.

Spring, J. (2000). *The universal right to education. Justification, definition, and guidelines*. Mahwah, NJ: Lawrence Erlbaum Associates.

Statman, D. (Ed.). (1993). *Moral luck*. Albany: State University of New York Press.

Stephenson, J., Ling, L., Burman, E., & Cooper, M. (Eds.). (1998). *Values in education*. London: Routledge.

Stevick, E. (1990). *Humanism in language teaching*. New York: Oxford University Press.

Stoll, D. (1982). *Fishers of men or founders of empire? The Wycliff bible translators in Latin America*. London: Zed.

Strauss, C., & Quinn, N. (1997). *A cognitive theory of cultural meaning*. Cambridge, England: Cambridge University Press.

Swales, J. (1987). Utilizing the literatures in teaching the research paper. *TESOL Quarterly, 21,* 41–68.

Tarone, E., & Allwright, D. (2001, May). *Language teacher-learning and student language-learning: Shaping the knowledge base.* Paper presented at the Second International Conference on Language Teacher Education, Minneapolis, MN.

Taylor, C. (1992). *The ethics of authenticity.* Cambridge, MA: Harvard University Press.

Teachers of English to Speakers of Other Languages. (2001). *Mission statement.* Accessed July 17, 2001, at http://www.tesol.org/mbr/whatis.html.

Tiffen, B. (1968). Language and education in Commonwealth Africa. In J. Dakin, D. Tiffen, & H. G. Widdowson (Eds.), *Language in education: The problem in Commonwealth Africa and the Indo–Pakistan sub-continent* (pp. 63–113). London: Oxford University Press.

Tippins, D. J., Tobin, K. G., & Hook, K. (1993). Ethical decisions at the heart of teaching: Making sense from a constructivist perspective. *Journal of Moral Education, 22,* 221–240.

Tom, A. (1984). *Teaching as a moral craft.* New York: Longman.

Torrance, H. (Ed.). (1995). *Evaluating authentic assessment.* Buckingham, England: Open University Press.

Torrance, H., & Pryor, J. (1998). *Investigating formative assessment: Teaching, learning, and assessment in the classroom.* Buckingham, England: Open University Press.

Tsui, A. B. M. (1996). Reticence and anxiety in second language learning. In K. M. Bailey & D. Nunan (Eds.), *Voices from the language classroom* (pp. 145–167). Cambridge, England: Cambridge University Press.

Universal Declaration of Human Rights. (1948). Accessed April 23, 2001, at http://www.udhr50.org/UDHR/default.htm.

Varghese, M. (2001a, February). *"La lengua es el espiritu del alma": Bilingual teachers as language planners.* Paper presented at the annual conference of the American Association for Applied Linguistics, St. Louis, MO.

Varghese, M. (2001b). Professional development as a site for the conceptualization and negotiation of bilingual teacher identities. In B. Johnston & S. Irujo (Eds.), *Research and practice in language teacher education: Voices from the field* (pp. 213–232). Minneapolis: University of Minnesota, Center for Advanced Research in Second Language Acquisition.

Wallace, M. J. (1998). *Action research for language teachers.* Cambridge, England: Cambridge University Press.

Wallraff, B. (2000, November). What global language? *Atlantic Monthly,* 52–66.

Weis, L., & Fine, M. (Eds.). (1993). *Beyond silenced voices: Class, race, and gender in United States schools.* Albany: State University of New York Press.

Welker, R. (1992). *The teacher as expert: A theoretical and historical examination.* Albany: State University of New York Press.

Whitehead, J. (1993). *The growth of educational knowledge: Creating your own living educational theories.* Bournemouth, England: Hyde.

Willett, J., & Jeannot, M. (1993). Resistance to taking a critical stance. *TESOL Quarterly, 27,* 477–495.

Willett, J., Solsken, J., & Wilson-Keenan, J. (1998). The (im)possibilities of constructing multicultural language practices in research and pedagogy. *Linguistics and Education, 10,* 165–218.

Wilson, J. (1988). *A preface to morality.* Totowa, NJ: Barnes & Noble.

Wink, J. (2000). *Critical pedagogy: Notes from the real world.* New York: Longman.

Witherell, C., & Noddings, N. (1991). *Stories lives tell: Narrative and dialogue in education.* New York: Teachers College Press.

Woods, D. (1996). *Teacher cognition in language teaching: Beliefs, decision-making, and classroom practice.* Cambridge, England: Cambridge University Press.

Woodward, T. (1991). *Models and metaphors in language teacher training: Loop input and other strategies.* Cambridge, England: Cambridge University Press.

Wosh, P. J. (1994). *Spreading the word: The Bible business in nineteenth-century America.* Ithaca, NY: Cornell University Press.

Yates, R., & Muchisky, D. (1999, May). *On the status of disciplinary knowledge in language teacher education.* Paper presented at the First International Conference on Language Teacher Education, Minneapolis, MN.

Zamel, V. (1982). Writing: The process of discovering meaning. *TESOL Quarterly, 16,* 195–210.

Zamel, V. (1983). The composing processes of advanced ESL students: Six case studies. *TESOL Quarterly, 17,* 165–187.

Author Index

A

Allwright, D., 121, 123, 125, 139, 152, 162
Amirault, C., 86, 152
Applebaum, B., 16, 147, 152
Argyris, C., 140, 152
Aschbacher, P.R., 82, 91, 156
Auerbach, E.R., 51, 61, 125, 152
Ayers, W., 100, 150, 152

B

Bachman, L.F., 76, 152
Bailey, K.M., 32, 152
Bakhtin, M.M., 108, 152
Ball, D.L., 16, 153
Ball, S.J., 50, 153
Barcelos, A.M., 103-106, 108, 117, 118, 146, 153
Bauman, Z., 14-15, 153
Benesch, S., 51, 61, 64, 153
Bentham, J., 12, 153
Bergem, T., 15, 153
Boostrom, R.E., 15, 16, 24, 25, 84, 157
Boshell, M., 123, 153
Bowers, B., 62, 73, 153
Branscombe, N.A., 125, 153
Breen, M.P., 34, 153
Brennan, M., 50, 160
Brown, H.D., 29, 153
Brumfit, C.J., 29, 155
Burman, E., 10, 161
Burns, A., 123, 124, 153
Buzzelli, C.A., 6, 9, 15, 16, 36, 153, 157
Byrnes, H., 89, 153

C

Cain, C., 6, 156
Canagarajah, S., 38, 51, 54, 153
Canale, M., 89, 153
Centre for British Teachers, 130, 153
Cole, D.J., 92, 154
Coleman, H., 51, 154
Colnerud, G., 16, 154
Cooper, M., 10, 161
Crookes, G., 61, 154

D

De Fina, A.A., 92, 154
Delpit, L., 34, 154
Dempsey, V.O., 15, 159
Dewey, J., 15, 154
Duff, P.A., 19, 99, 154
DuFon, M., 17, 154

E

Eastman, C.M., 154
Edge, J., 10, 17, 32, 51, 18, 114, 116, 117, 121, 123, 144, 145, 146, 147, 148, 154
Edstam, T.S., 106, 134, 154
Eggington, W.G., 51, 156
Eisenberg, J.A., 12, 154
Eison, J.A., 80, 159
Elbow, P., 41, 155
Emig, J., 41, 155
Ephron, S., 16, 158

165

Subject Index